A Priest in the Family

A Priest in the Family

A Guide for Parents Whose Sons Are Considering Priesthood

By Fr. Brett A. Brannen

VIANNEY VOCATIONS

Rev. Brett Brannen is a priest of the Catholic Diocese of Savannah, Georgia, where he served as Vocation Director for ten years. He also served as Vice-Rector of Mount St. Mary's Seminary in Emmitsburg, Maryland.

Vianney Vocations LLC, Valdosta, Georgia 31601
© 2014 by Brett A. Brannen
All rights reserved.
Printed in the United States of America

ISBN: 978-0-9896212-2-9

LCCN: 2014944106

Nihil obstat: Rev. Douglas K. Clark, STL
Imprimatur: Most Rev. Gregory J. Hartmayer, OFM Conv., D.D.,
Diocese of Savannah

Cover photo by Graham Tidy of The Canberra Times, featuring Rev. Paul Nulley and family.

To the Most Blessed Mother Mary and to St. Joseph,
her Blessed Spouse,
the parents of the First Priest

CONTENTS

FOREWORD

If you have picked up this book, it is probably because a young man in whom you are *invested* — your son, grandson, brother, or nephew — is thinking about the priesthood.

I can relate on a few levels. My husband Gary and I are the parents of a seminarian and so we probably have similar concerns as you. We're happy for our son, but are highly aware that he has a long road ahead of him, and that he may or may not be ordained a priest.

I also have another perspective. For several years I have worked with Vocation Offices all over the country. (These are the diocesan offices that help aspiring priests.) In this capacity, I talk with many other parents about their sons' vocations. Some are thrilled that their sons are considering priesthood, some not so thrilled, and some even adamantly opposed. But they let me into the conversation. I feel most blessed to work with parents who are supportive, but frightened because they feel spiritually inadequate. They ask themselves, "How can we support our son's vocation when we ourselves don't fully understand the priesthood or seminary?" Part of my job is *demystifying* these realities for them — which is precisely Fr. Brannen's purpose in this book.

Today's parents raise their children differently than my parents or my grandparents. In previous generations, children gained a level of autonomy at younger ages. Today, many of us are intimately involved with our children's interests, whether soccer, violin, or social media. Frequently these hands-on parenting relationships last into the late teens and early twenties. These days, the age of eighteen does not equal instantaneous independence.

Thus if your son's interest in priesthood comes as something of a surprise, it's possible that you may feel suddenly left out of the decision-making process. You may see your son developing a relationship with the vocation director and feel a certain sense of abandonment. You want to know what your son is getting into, and rightfully so.

It's helpful to know that the vocation director is not a recruiter. The Church does not want to steal your son. In fact, the vocation director wants exactly the same thing as you — he wants the best for your son, which is embracing God's call, whatever it may be. His job is simply to help your son to turn off the noise of life in order to hear the whisper of God.

But that does not mean you will no longer be needed. My strongest consolation for parents of aspiring priests is this: *You are not alone! We are doing this together, and we are doing it with God.* Working with your son and the Church, you can offer tremendous support as a parent. Discernment is not meant to be a solitary endeavor; your son needs you and your prayers as he continues to seek the will of God.

It does take a certain generosity of spirit to let go of your son should he attend seminary. As the parents of four children, my husband and I have learned that Catholic parenting means learning to trust in God's plan, not ours. We remind ourselves that God's call for our children may be different than his call for us.

As you will see, Fr. Brannen clearly has a gift for writing about God's call to the priesthood. He is able to anticipate parents' concerns, then explain with clarity and joy what priesthood is all about. This is an amazingly thorough volume, answering nearly every question I ever heard a parent ask. When you come to the last page, I think you will be much more peaceful, and dare I say *excited*, about the prospect of having a priest in the family.

Mrs. Rosemary Sullivan
Executive Director of the National Conference of Diocesan Vocation Directors
August 2014

ACKNOWLEDGEMENTS

I wish to acknowledge with gratitude my own parents, Bob and Sylvia Brannen, who have supported me in so many ways throughout my life and my vocation. I am grateful to them for teaching me two very important things about life. My mother taught me about Jesus Christ and my faith, and my father taught me the value of hard work.

Many thanks to the vocation directors, rectors, parents of priests, and many others who generously read the first draft of this book and offered invaluable feedback: Fr. Timothy McKeown, Vice Rector of the North American College in Rome; Msgr. Steven Rohlfs, Rector of Mount St. Mary's Seminary in Maryland; Fr. John Horn, S.J., Rector of Kenrick-Glennon Seminary in St. Louis; Fr. Tim Birney, Vocation Director in Detroit; Fr. Sam Kachuba, Vocation Director in Bridgeport; Fr. J.D. Jaffe, Vocation Director in Arlington; Fr. Rich Gabuzda, Director of the Institute for Priestly Formation in Omaha; Jack and Judy Cozzens, parents of Bishop Andrew Cozzens of Minneapolis-St. Paul; Mike and Beverly Firmin, parents of Fr. Daniel Firmin, Vicar General of the Diocese of Savannah, Sean Yeo and Lucy Chew, of Serra International in Singapore; Sr. Ellen Marie Hagar, D.C., President of Elizabeth Seton High School in Maryland; Susan Massey, Serra Club of Houston; and Rosemary Sullivan, Executive Director of the National Conference of Diocesan Vocation Directors.

I want to especially acknowledge and thank Mr. Mike Pettit, the father of Fr. Neil Pettit of the Diocese of Lafayette, Louisiana. I met Mike during a Family Weekend when I was Vice Rector at Mount St. Mary's Seminary and he stayed in touch through the years. He was the instrument of the Holy Spirit in moving me to write this book!

I am grateful for all of those who helped with the editing process. Thanks to Colleen Brannen, my sister in law, for her meticulous proofreading of the final manuscript. I thank Colleen for sharing this great gift.

I acknowledge, with gratitude to God, Mr. Sam Alzheimer, President of Vianney Vocations. He is the primary and chief editor of this work, and the publisher as well. Sam and I worked together very closely on this book, just as we did on my first book, *To Save a Thousand Souls.* He believed that this book was greatly needed in the Church and that it would be a valuable asset for the parents and family of seminarians and priests. When I presented the idea to him, he encouraged me to write and agreed to once again serve as editor. Sam's knowledge of discernment and priestly vocations was extraordinarily valuable during the writing and editing process.

Finally, I want to acknowledge the parents and family members of all seminarians and priests. You have made many sacrifices to raise your son. Now may Jesus raise your son to the altar as a priest!

INTRODUCTION

"As he was walking by the Sea of Galilee, Jesus saw two
brothers, Simon who is called Peter, and his brother
Andrew, casting a net into the sea; they were fishermen.
He said to them, "Come after me, and I will make you
fishers of men." At once they left their nets and
followed him. He walked along from there and saw two
other brothers, James, the son of Zebedee, and his
brother John. They were in a boat, with their father
Zebedee, mending their nets. He called them, and
immediately they left their boat and their father and
followed him."

Matthew 4:18-22

I often think about Zebedee! He was an honest man trying to
make an honest living in the family fishing business with his two
sons. Then Jesus walked by, called James and John, and they left
Zebedee alone in the boat mending his tangled nets. Can you
relate to this story?

"Father, my son wants to be a priest and I have so many
questions, emotions, and concerns." I have heard this comment,
or a similar one, many times through the years. Perhaps your son
is very young and just beginning to think about priesthood.
Maybe he has just graduated from college and made the decision
to give seminary a try. Or maybe your son is already a priest, but
you still have some lingering, unanswered questions. Whatever
your situation, this book was written for you.

I have been a priest for twenty-three years and I served as
vocation director for the Diocese of Savannah and vice rector of
Mount St. Mary's Seminary in Emmitsburg, Maryland for sixteen
of those years. In these two positions, I worked with hundreds of
seminarians on a day-to-day basis. I also met and interacted with
many of their parents and relatives who had sincere questions
and concerns. Some were happier than others about their sons'
interest in the priesthood. All of them greatly desired that their
sons would be happy and fulfilled.

One such parent, the father of a newly ordained priest,
found that he was serving as a counselor to other parents whose

sons were considering seminary. He had read my book, *To Save a Thousand Souls,* and was trying his best to address his friends' questions, but he was unsure of many answers. He sent me a long email explaining the need for a book for parents of future priests. That was the impetus I needed to start writing.

In my experience, once parents and family members receive good, accurate answers to their questions, even if they are not initially excited about the answers, at least they are in a better position to dialogue with their son about his decision. Popular media has spread a great deal of misinformation about priests, so I hope that this book will offer a more accurate depiction of seminary and priesthood.

This book is written to be read sequentially, chapter by chapter, to take you through the many questions and concerns that most parents or relatives have. There is also an appendix of questions to which you can refer, perhaps to answer your most pressing questions first. I have tried to address common issues thoroughly, but succinctly, not offering too much information. If you want more information about a certain topic, I refer you to the Recommended Reading appendix. I have also placed a section between every chapter entitled "Parents, Priests, and Providence." These are short anecdotes about the parent-priest relationships of different priests, some of them famous saints.

You will notice that I will often use the phrase "your son" when writing about a man considering priesthood. The book is certainly written with parents in mind, but it is also useful for other family members, relatives, and friends. Also, please note that this book primarily addresses diocesan priesthood. Some of my observations would not be applicable if your son plans to become a priest in a religious order such as the Franciscans, Jesuits, or Dominicans (though likely you still will find some chapters to be helpful).

It is interesting that the wife of Zebedee and the mother of James and John (whose name is thought to have been Salome), was also a disciple of Jesus. She, the mother of these two disciples, is the one who approached Jesus in Matthew 20:20-28 to ask if her two sons could sit on his right and on his left when he entered into his Kingdom. It was a request that showed she did not really understand the fullness of Jesus' message, even though she knew him, loved him, and followed him.

If as a parent you feel like Zebedee or his wife—left alone questioning your son's call—I hope this book will help untangle the nets, so to speak, and give you a measure of peace.

Fr. Brett Brannen
August 2014

"I don't think you're thinking what I'm thinking."

CHAPTER 1

"MOM AND DAD, I HAVE GREAT NEWS!"

I very clearly remember the night in 1984 when I first told my father that I was going to the seminary. I had already discussed my interest in priesthood with my mother. She is a devout Catholic who attends daily Mass, so she was excited and supportive. My father, on the other hand, was a non-practicing Baptist who had little information about Catholicism other than what he had gleaned from watching his wife and children practice their faith. He was not at all happy, even though he already suspected I was interested in the priesthood. He loudly and angrily blamed our local pastor, a priest whom, ironically, my father liked and respected greatly.

At that tense moment, I reminded my dad of something he had said repeatedly to me and my siblings as we grew up: "You can do anything you want with your life, but I expect you to do your very best. As long as you give it your all, I will support you no matter what you choose." Calming down a bit, he acknowledged that he had said this often. So I said, "Well, this is what I have chosen, and I promise you that I will be the very best priest that I can be. I am asking you to support me." And my father, who is a man of his word, accepted my decision.

Twenty-three years later, both of my parents are proud that I am a Catholic priest. My father is still Baptist technically, but he attends Mass every Sunday with my mother and the grandchildren. I have two brothers and one sister who have always supported my vocation. They joke that I am their ticket to heaven because God knew this crazy family needed a priest. My younger brother often remarks that God sent him one brother, a lawyer, to keep him out of jail and another brother, a priest, to keep him out of hell!

As "the family priest," it has been my privilege to baptize all ten of my nieces and nephews, and to walk with them as they grow in faith. One day I hope to have the honor of witnessing their marriage vows, should they be called to marriage. I thank God for the wonderful gift of the family he has given to me.

While my parents are now comfortable with me being a priest, your emotional reaction about your son's interest in the priesthood may be quite different. Perhaps, like my mother, you are excited and proud. But honestly, you may be neither excited nor proud. Perhaps, like my father, you are upset about this news.

The following statements illustrate where different parents find themselves on the emotional spectrum. Which of these most closely reflects your sentiments?

~ I could not be happier that my son wants to become a priest! I have prayed for years that someone in our family would have a vocation to priesthood, so I am thrilled that God has answered my prayers. I love my son and I am proud of him. I can't wait to visit him in seminary.

~ I love my Catholic faith, I love the priests in my parish, and I love my son. I am excited that he might become a priest. However, I am worried about many things and I have so many questions. Can he really do this? Will he be happy? Is this really God's plan?

~ I respect priests and the good work they do, but I don't understand why they have to be celibate. It just doesn't seem normal. Priesthood would not have been my first choice for my son, but I love him and I will support him if this is what he wants.

~ I really do not know what to think about this! My son's interest in the priesthood caught me completely by surprise. I know very little about what a priest does. When he told me he was going to seminary, my first reaction was disbelief, and I still feel uneasy about it.

~ I am shocked by this news. I was hoping that my son would marry, give me grandchildren, and have a normal life. He is so bright. I am not in favor of his decision because I think he will be unhappy in the long run. I wish he would reconsider.

~ I am very much against this decision. I have done my best to discourage my son from going to seminary. I have read so many terrible things that priests have done, and I don't want him to be labeled as a child abuser. I don't even know what

2

priests are supposed to do! Why would anyone
want to give up so much?

As you can see, some parents have been hoping and praying
for years that one of their sons would become a priest. Others are
devastated and feel that they have lost their son. Most parents are
somewhere in between: perhaps feeling somewhat proud that he
would pursue such a generous life, but concerned, worried, and
in need of answers.

One mother told me, "Priesthood is something so out-of-the-
ordinary; it just does not seem normal." She was right. Priesthood
is an extraordinary vocation and a difficult one to understand
and accept. It is all the more difficult when the parents struggle
with their own faith. But even peaceful, practicing Catholic
parents can struggle. Another parent of a twenty-year-old
seminarian said to me, "You know, I have dutifully prayed for
vocations at Mass for years, but that was for someone else's son!
Now that it is my son, I'm not so sure."

It is understandable that parents and relatives might have a
hard time digesting this news, especially if it comes as a complete
surprise. Because the priesthood is such an uncommon vocation,
most parents don't know how to react. For example, on hearing
the news from her son, a surprised mother may start asking
strongly-worded questions in rapid fire. Such an exchange can be
very intimidating to her son, who himself may not have a full
understanding of the priesthood yet.

Seminarians have often told me that having this "talk" with
their parents was a stressful encounter that caused them great
anxiety. Some dreaded their parents' reaction for weeks before
they broke the news. Why? Because they genuinely felt God's call
and wanted to be affirmed. They knew that their decision to
apply for seminary was counter-cultural, so they craved
validation from loved ones, but they suspected that their parents
would be skeptical.

I love the anecdote that someone emailed me a few years
back. I have adapted it for this topic.

A clever young man in his final year of college emailed
his parents in November. This is what he wrote:

"Dear mom and dad, I am writing to tell you why I will
not be coming home for Christmas this year. I had a
wreck the other night and my car is badly damaged.

Besides a broken arm, I am fine. I do not have the money to repair the car, as I had to use it to bail my roommate out of jail. I have had to take a job at a local fast food restaurant and they cannot give me time off to come home at Christmas. I need the money so I have to work. Having to work so many hours is affecting my grades, but I think I am going to pass some of my classes. Finally, I have a new girlfriend and we are thinking about getting married soon. I will tell you about that later. Other than that, I am doing fine. Merry Christmas and I hope to see you soon.

"P.S. Actually, mom and dad, I did not have a wreck and I have no broken bones. My roommate was never in jail. I am not working at a fast food restaurant and I am doing great in all my classes. I do not have a girlfriend, I do not plan to get married, and I am coming home for Christmas. And after graduation, I am applying to the seminary to become a priest… and I hope that you will see this news in the proper perspective."

Even though applying to seminary is big news, your son could be doing many other things that would be big news, but not good news. To be called to be a priest of Jesus Christ is a great honor and privilege. It truly is good news!

It is critical to understand that *going to seminary is not a final decision to become a priest.* (I would have written that sentence in red, but this book is printed in black and white!) Your son is not "signing in blood" that he will become a priest. He is simply responding to the call, as he perceives it, to give seminary the ol' college try, one year at a time.

Seminary is a period of intensive discernment, and men who are in seminary frequently discern they are *not* called to priesthood. Typically a man has six to eight years to decide. (Compare that to dating and marriage!) In college seminary, *only about half* the students finish the philosophy program, go on to theology, and finally advance to ordination. Once in major seminary (the last four years), approximately *three-quarters* of seminarians go on to become priests.

Whether you are excited that your son is going to seminary or not, you must admit that he is a very good, generous man to even consider priesthood. Whether he ends up becoming a priest or not, the fact that he is willing to try says a great deal about his faith, character, and integrity. Tell your son that you will do your best to support him and to help him in this journey of continued discernment and study. And tell him that you will do your part to become better informed about the mystery of God's call to priesthood. Tell your son that you love him very much.

People may soon be saying to you, "Congratulations! You must be so proud that your son is going to the seminary to become a priest!" Truthfully, it is a great honor for a man to be chosen by God to be a priest, however you may feel at present.

This really is great news! But I know you still have questions and concerns.

Keep reading.

Parents, Priests, and Providence

Pope Francis's Mother Surprised by His Vocation

In an interview with a Spanish-language newspaper[1], Pope Francis's only living sibling, María Elena Bergoglio, recounts how their mother discovered he was interested in the priesthood.

At age nineteen, young Jorge Bergoglio initially felt that he wanted to study medicine. Wanting him to have a quiet place to study, his mother prepared a special room for him by cleaning out a cluttered room on the family's terrace.

One day, the future pope's mother entered the room to clean it. But she ran into a surprise: books of theology.

The pope's sister recounted the conversation between mother and son:

"Jorge, come here. You told me that you were going to study medicine."

"Yes, mother."

"Why did you lie to me?"

"No, I did not lie to you, mother; I am going to study the medicine of the soul."

Surprised by the news, his mother wept, because she understood he would have to leave home to study. His father, however, rejoiced in his son's vocation.

Eventually the entire family embraced his call to the priesthood. Jorge Bergoglio was ordained a priest in 1969 and elected Pope in 2013.

CHAPTER 2

WHY WOULD ANYONE WANT TO BE A PRIEST?

There is an apocryphal story told about Jesus speaking with one of his angels as they looked down at the earth. The angel said, "Lord, I am looking at a world covered in darkness but I see a few lights. What are those twelve tiny lights I see?" Jesus replied, "Those lights are my eleven disciples and my mother. It is my plan that those twelve lights will spread my love, my grace, and my teaching to every person who will ever live." The angel kept staring at the earth and after a few minutes said, "Lord, there sure is a lot of darkness down there. What if it doesn't work? What is Plan B?" And the Lord Jesus replied, "There is no Plan B."

Why would anyone want to be a priest? To put it simply, God calls some men to become priests because the priesthood is an important part of the plan of Jesus to save the world.

The priesthood of Jesus Christ is a radical life. It requires sacrifices that many people in this world perceive to be foolish. One father asked his son: "Why do you want to do this? Why do you want to listen to other people's problems all the time? Why give up marriage, sex, and your own children? Why choose to be poor? Why on earth would anyone want to do this?"

The short answer is because God has called him to do this. Priests can be very powerful instruments in the hands of Jesus to help bring people to Heaven. As Catholics, we believe that God himself created some men, with the help of their parents (whom Pope St. John Paul II called "co-creators"), with the specific intention that they will become priests. It is God who places the desire for priesthood into a man's mind and heart, and it is often unexplainable even to the man himself.

Sure, there are scenarios when a man wants to be a priest for the wrong reasons. This kind of man, though, typically never makes it into seminary, or if he does, he does not stay very long. By and large, most men go through a prayerful process of gathering information and consulting trustworthy priests. Very often, men even wish God were *not* calling them to the priesthood. So chances are, if your son announces that he wants to be a priest, the call could be genuine. Jesus said, "You did not choose me but I chose you."

7

If God is calling your son, he will give him the grace to live his priesthood with happiness and joy — even while sacrificing those things that the world so often equates with fulfillment.

The purpose of a priest is to bring people to Jesus and Jesus to people.

An Encounter with Jesus

Pope Francis writes, in his encyclical *Evangelii Gaudium* (The Joy of the Gospel): "I invite all Christians, everywhere, at this very moment, to a renewed encounter with Jesus Christ...I ask all of you to do this unfailingly each day. No one should think this invitation is not meant for him or her, since no one is excluded from the joy brought by the Lord."

Your son has had a personal encounter with this Jesus and he has fallen in love with Him! Jesus is irresistible, for those who have come to know Him, and his call is powerful for those who love Him. There are (approximately) four hundred thousand Catholic priests in the world today who follow Jesus joyfully, making all of the required sacrifices! How do they do this? Why? Because they have fallen in love with the Master and He gives them the grace to do what they have been called to do. And they do it with joy!

Ask your son to tell you about his personal encounter with the Lord Jesus, the time or times when he was overwhelmed with the Lord's love and goodness. If he had not had this experience, he would not be thinking of priesthood.

Priests Are Happy

Many studies about happiness have been conducted over the years. One profession consistently ranks number one for personal happiness: clergy. Contrary to what many in secular society would assume, Catholic priests overwhelmingly report that they are happy and fulfilled.

A number of books have been written about this phenomenon. Here is a revealing passage from Msgr. Stephen J. Rossetti, a leading researcher on priesthood:

> "In my most recent survey of 2,441 priests around the United States, an astounding 92.2% said they were happy as priests;

88.6% said their morale was good; 93.2% said they feel a
sense of closeness to God; and 94.8% said they feel a joy that
is a grace from God."[2]

So why are priests so happy? A loving God would never call
a man only to abandon him. God will never send us where his
grace cannot sustain us. God is infinite in power and he made all
people for happiness and fulfillment. He made us to give
ourselves generously as a gift. Whenever a person does this, he is
happy and fulfilled. I think this is especially true for priests,
because Jesus Christ instituted the priesthood precisely so that
priests would serve others with their entire lives.

What Kind of Man Goes to the Seminary?

Your son wants to go to the seminary because he suspects,
based on evidence from inside and outside of his heart, that God
has created him specifically to serve as a priest.

What is this evidence? What are these signs? They are best
described as *insights* which he has gathered from his prayer,
service, life experience, and study. Most seminarians will say
something like: "I just feel in my gut that this is the right thing for
me; to go to the seminary and give it a try. I can really see myself
happy as a priest."

Below are three hypothetical scenarios illustrating the wide
variety of men who feel called to the priesthood. As you'll see,
there is no standard mold; God calls all kinds. These stories are
based on my experience reading the autobiographies of hundreds
of young men who went to seminary and eventually became
priests. See if you recognize your son in these scenarios.

Scenario 1: John

John was raised in the Catholic Church with his brothers and
sisters and attended Mass faithfully with his family. Though he
was a normal boy in every way — playful, athletic, sometimes lazy
with his school work, fighting with his siblings — there seemed to
be something different about him. During Mass, he would stare
at the priest and listen intently to the homily. He would ask very
perceptive spiritual questions on the drive home from Mass,
questions that his parents often could not answer. Clearly he was
thinking deeply about his faith.

John became an altar boy in fourth grade and later joined the youth group. His mother would sometimes see him making the sign of the cross when an ambulance passed by, something he had learned in Catholic school. In high school, he played sports and dated, but he continued to be prayerful. For some strange reason which even he could not understand, he just liked being around the church.

Some months, and some years, he was more religious than others, but he kept coming back, going to confession, Mass, and Eucharistic adoration. In college, he started attending a Bible study at the Catholic campus ministry, and through those contacts, went on a mission trip to Mexico. When he returned, John became good friends with several priests on campus and in his hometown and they invited him to consider becoming a priest himself. These priests knew the signs and they could see that John might very well have a vocation to priesthood. As this desire continued to grow, John read more books about priesthood and discernment. He went on retreats and spent quite a bit of time visiting web sites about priesthood. He started going to daily Mass and frequent spiritual direction. The devout, elderly ladies who attended daily Mass in the parish began to tell him, "You know, you would make a great priest."

Scenario 2: Ryan

Ryan was never a pious boy. Quite the opposite: he seemed to be always in trouble. He was loud, hyperactive, and rough, and his comments often hurt people's feelings. When challenged about his behavior, he seemed sincerely sorry. But the behavior would not stop. He was athletic and aggressive, and much preferred to be outside playing football to anything like school or church.

In high school, Ryan rebelled strongly and stopped going to Mass. He became sexually active with several girlfriends and drank frequently, behaviors which got even worse in college. He was a handsome man, fit and muscular, with a gregarious personality. Women were very attracted to him.

In his third year of college, he met a girl named Catherine, for whom he fell hard. She was a devout Catholic. She was beautiful, intelligent, and virtuous. She refused to act impurely with Ryan. He was inspired by her goodness, attracted to her real beauty, and fell in love with her. As his friends said, "Catherine is the kind of girl you want to take home to mom."

Because he wanted to impress her, Ryan started going to Mass with her. At her encouragement, he even went to confession. A true conversion began to happen in his heart, and for the first time in his life, he began to think deeply about Jesus and what He had done for us. He felt sorry that he had taken Jesus for granted for so many years. His parents were extremely pleased at the change they saw in him. He would go to Mass daily, both at school and when he was home for the holidays, and they could see he was striving to live a genuine life of virtue. They thanked God for Catherine, and had every hope and expectation that she would become Ryan's wife.

At Christmas in his fourth year of college, Ryan told both Catherine and his parents that he wanted to become a priest. His parents were shocked and disappointed! In her goodness, though it caused her great pain, Catherine could see that he may be called to be a priest. She had the wisdom to understand that he would never be able to commit himself completely to her in marriage until he had given seminary a try.

Scenario 3: Dominic

Dominic was never into sports. He was quiet and shy, a bit overweight, and not very aggressive, unlike many of his peers. He much preferred playing computer games and staying indoors to doing anything outside. He was an average student, and although he passed all of his subjects, he never really seemed to be very excited about any of them. His parents worried about Dominic during his early years in school. He was not very popular with his peers and he did not really seem to fit into any one group. His mother kept saying, "We just need to find something that Dominic is good at, and that will boost his self-confidence." Nonetheless, he was a congenial boy and he never got into any trouble. He never griped or complained about anything. It was clear that he had a good heart. He went to Sunday Mass with the family faithfully and said his night prayers, but other than that, did not show much interest in his faith.

Then in seventh grade, a missionary priest wearing a black habit came to visit his Catholic school and talked about bringing Jesus to tribal people in strange, foreign lands. This impressed

Dominic so much that he even wrote an English paper about foreign missionaries. During high school, Dominic became more and more active in the parish. He began to serve Mass, something he had declined to do earlier because of his timidity. He joined the youth group, which became his primary social circle. He went on several retreats and service trips led by an energetic youth minister.

Dominic became "a church mouse," and seemed to be there every time the doors were unlocked. Some of the pious older ladies remarked to his parents that he would make a good priest. Then, at the beginning of his senior year of high school, Dominic spoke to his parents about becoming a priest. He had been speaking with the pastor and going to spiritual direction, and the pastor had encouraged Dominic to consider a college seminary. His parents were concerned about this, because he had never even been on a date, but they were so happy to see him excited about something and moving in a positive direction, they decided to give him their blessing.

Most parents will see some similarities between one or more of these scenarios and their own son's life. Jesus orchestrates a man's life by sending certain people and events into his path, along with certain graces, which combine to become part of God's call to priesthood.

"To every man, there comes in his lifetime that special moment when he is physically tapped on the shoulder and offered the chance to do a very special thing, unique to him and fitted to his talent; what a tragedy if that moment finds him unprepared or unqualified for the work which would be his finest hour."

Winston Churchill

2013 U.S. Ordination Class

It is always interesting to read the annual statistics gleaned by CARA, The Center for Applied Research in the Apostolate, regarding the men ordained priests each year in the U.S. The annual report shows us some of the qualities, habits, interests, and influences in the men who are ordained. It may be helpful to see how these factors compare or contrast with your son's background.

In 2013, approximately 500 men were ordained priests. The following statistics are based on their answers to CARA's survey.[3]

~ On average, more than 90 percent of the men in the ordination class were baptized as infants. Fewer than 10 percent became Catholic later in life.

~ Around 80 percent indicated that both parents are Catholic, and more than a third have a relative who is a priest or religious.

~ The average age at which they first considered a vocation to priesthood was seventeen. An impressive 67 percent say they were encouraged to consider priesthood by another priest. Others who encouraged them include friends (46 percent), parishioners (38 percent) and mothers (34 percent).

~ About 67 percent of those ordained report their primary race or ethnicity as Caucasian/European American/white. Three in ten were born outside the United States, with the largest numbers coming from Mexico, Vietnam, Colombia, Poland, the Philippines, and Nigeria.

~ More than half of the Class of 2013 have more than two siblings, while one in five have five or more siblings. Ordinands, the men ordained priests, are likely to be the oldest in their family (40 percent).

~ Before entering the seminary, 63 percent completed college. Almost one quarter (23 percent) entered the seminary with a graduate degree. One in three entered the seminary while in college.

~ Two-thirds indicated they served as an altar server and about half participated in a parish youth group. Around 20 percent participated in a World Youth Day before entering the seminary.

~ Around 42 percent attended a Catholic elementary school, (a rate equal to that for all Catholic adults in the United States).

~ Ordinands are somewhat more likely than other U.S. Catholic adults to have attended a Catholic high school and they are much more likely to have attended a Catholic college (44 percent attended Catholic College).

~ Many ordinands had a full-time work experience prior to entering the seminary, most often in education, accounting, finance, or insurance. Four percent served in the U.S. Armed Forces at some point.

~ The survey also found that about a quarter of new priests have educational debt, averaging just over $20,000.

I am sure that you can see some parallels and some differences in these statistics, in comparison to your son's life and discernment. However, please notice that these men all had important experiences in family, education, religion, service, and prayer. God uses all of a man's experiences when he is calling him to be a priest, but the man must still make a careful "discernment." What exactly does discernment mean?

What is a Diligent Discernment?

In the hypothetical scenarios above, John, Ryan, and Dominic all had a prolonged period of *discernment*: a time for evaluating the evidence in their lives, with the help of others, to see if priesthood might be their true vocation. These insights are gathered through prayer, service, life experience, and study, all under the influence of God's grace. Some of these insights are in their intellects and others are in their hearts. I call this a Diligent Discernment.

The word diligent comes from the Latin word *diligere*. It means to love and to choose after careful study. The word discernment comes from the Latin word *discernere*, which means to separate by sifting; to distinguish between. So making a diligent discernment means, especially for a young man, the following:

1. The man has looked very carefully at the option of priesthood.
2. He has gathered correct information about discernment and priesthood.
3. He has prayed about the call to go to the seminary consistently over an extensive period of time.
4. He has spoken regularly with a spiritual director and his vocation director.
5. He has discussed his discernment with his parents and carefully considered their counsel (especially if he is young).
6. He feels peace about this decision in his heart and that peace has remained.
7. His vocation director has given him permission to apply.

Number 7 is very important. The man must discern with the help of the local vocation director. A man cannot discern diocesan priesthood without the Church. The vocation director is the priest to whom the bishop has assigned this task. Therefore, there are actually two discernments going on at the same time. The man is discerning if he should go to the seminary and if he is ready for that step. And the vocation director is discerning if this man should become a priest and if he is ready to begin seminary. The bishop is the spiritual father of every Catholic in the diocese and he wants to make sure that this young man has not been unduly influenced. He and the vocation director will make sure that your son has indeed made a diligent discernment.

Your son should have had a similar experience of discernment before he goes to seminary. If through this process his desire to be a priest has grown stronger, eventually he will reach a point where he needs to go to seminary to "test" his call. He is not absolutely sure he will become a priest, but he is sure that he should give seminary a try.

"You did not choose me but I chose you, and appointed you that you would go and bear fruit, and that your fruit would remain, so that whatever you ask of the Father in my name he may give to you."

John 15:16

Remember that this was not your son's idea! This call comes from God, and your son, hearing that call, has to give an answer. That answer may be yes. It may be no. It may be yes, but not yet. By definition, a vocation is a request from God, an invitation. It is not a commandment. Your son is still free. He is not being coerced by the Almighty to do something he does not want to do. He is always free to say no, but in fact, he *wants* to go to seminary. For now, at least, he sees the vocation of priesthood as the way he can be most happy and fulfilled in his life. He has evidence in his life, along with an internal conviction, that he should further explore this call in seminary.

"Amos answered Amaziah, 'I am not a prophet, nor do I belong to a company of prophets. I am a herdsman and a dresser of sycamores, but the Lord took me from following the flock, and the Lord said to me, "Go, prophesy to my people Israel."'"

Amos 7:14

Three Levels of Vocation

The word *vocation* is derived from the Latin *vocare*, to call. Note that in the aforementioned case studies, each young man first had a genuine encounter with Jesus that deepened his faith. This brings up a very important point, namely, that the first and highest vocation is always the same. *Everyone* is called to be holy, to become like Jesus, to be a saint. We are put on this earth to learn to love in the way that everyone loves in heaven. Thus *holiness* is everyone's primary vocation.

Priesthood, religious life, and marriage are actually secondary vocations. They are "states of life" in which a person has the highest chance of accomplishing his first vocation. In my own case, since God called me (knowing and loving me even before the creation of the world) to be a priest, my absolute best chance to become a saint is in the vocation of priesthood. Though I certainly could have gotten married and raised a family, becoming a saint in the vocation of marriage would have been more difficult for me.

I explain it to the grade school children in my parish this way: I am a round peg in a round hole. God made me this way and that is why I am so happy as a priest. If a person is called to the vocation of Holy Marriage, then it is in marriage that he has the best chance for sanctity. But if a person chooses a vocation to which God is *not* calling him, then he will be like a square peg in a round hole. Holiness, and therefore happiness, will be more difficult for him to attain. I do not say that it is impossible. But it is more difficult.

"The only success recognized by God is Christ-likeness."

Pope St. John Paul II

There is yet a third level of vocation, which we more commonly refer to as an *occupation*. For example, we all know that some teachers have magnificent gifts for imparting knowledge to young people, and we admire those teachers greatly. We may even say of a teacher, "She has found her vocation."

It is important to distinguish one's secondary vocation (priesthood or marriage, for example) from occupation (teacher or lawyer). If a man is called to the vocation of marriage, he must still discern his occupation. He must ask himself how to use his God-given gifts to support his family and build the Kingdom of God. But if a man is called to be a diocesan priest, he already knows that he will be very well-occupied taking care of God's people. Thus to be called to diocesan priesthood is to make two very important decisions simultaneously — one's vocation and one's occupation. A diocesan priest has no time to practice law or medicine or engineering. His full time work is caring for souls and bringing people in his parish to Jesus Christ. (Note that this is not true for religious priests, who can have a very wide variety of assignments ranging from missionary to college professor.)

Every vocation is about using the specific gifts God has given to you in order to help Jesus bring other people to Heaven. In the mystical Body of Christ, God never gives gifts to one person for himself alone. He gives gifts to one person for the salvation of other people!

We have examined why a man may find himself desiring to become a priest. As I wrote in the beginning of this chapter, the priesthood of Jesus Christ is a radical life. This is true. But the word *radical* actually means *rooted*. Your son is deeply rooted in his faith. He believes in Jesus Christ. He believes in the Catholic Church. And he has evidence that God is calling him to serve Jesus and his Church in a powerful way as a priest. He desires to freely give his life as a gift to others, to help them come to know and serve this same Sovereign Lord. There is great joy in this!

"I have told you this so that my joy may be in you and your joy may be complete. This is my commandment: love one another as I love you. No one has greater love than this, to lay down one's life for one's friends."

John 15:11-13

The Mother of St. Maximillian Kolbe

Three times that very day, his mother had said to him, "Raymond, stop running around the house so wildly. You are going to break something or hurt someone." The little boy continued his energetic play until he came flying around the corner and ran into his mother, her arms full of dishes. The dishes came crashing to the floor. In exasperation, she said, "Raymond, I told you to calm down. Now look what you have done." Shaking her head, she added, "What will ever become of you?"

The boy put his head down in shame and walked to the back of the house. There was a small shrine there, with an altar and a statue of the Blessed Virgin. He knelt before it and said, "Blessed Mother, what *will* ever become of me?"

That very night, he had a vision of the Blessed Virgin who came to him holding two crowns, one white and the other red. She asked him if he was willing to accept either of these crowns. The white crown meant that he should persevere in purity and the red crown that he should be a martyr. He said that he wanted both.

Raymond Kolbe grew up to become a Franciscan priest, ordained in 1919, and was given the religious name Maximillian. He began an organization called the Militia Immaculata (Army of Mary), to work for the conversion of sinners and enemies of the Church. He also preached missions in Japan and established a friary there.

In 1941, back in Poland, he was arrested by the Nazis and sent to the concentration camp at Auschwitz. After three Jewish prisoners escaped, the Nazi officers selected ten more prisoners at random to be killed in the starvation bunker. One cried out, "My wife, my children!" Fr. Kolbe volunteered to take his place. In the prison cell, he sang hymns and encouraged the other prisoners. After two weeks with no food or water, he was the only one still alive, so the guards injected him with carbolic acid. He died a martyr. St. Maximillian Kolbe was canonized by Pope John Paul II in 1982. He received both the white crown of purity and the red crown of martyrdom.

His mother had asked a great question: "What will ever become of you?"

CHAPTER 3

WHAT EXACTLY DOES A PRIEST DO?

When I received the phone call, my heart fell. One of our young parishioners, just sixteen years old, had committed suicide. He had shot himself in the head with a deer rifle. The police wanted me to come to the family's home immediately. I drove to the house praying that the Holy Spirit would give me the words to say and the wisdom to know what to do. When I pulled up, several family members came running out to my car crying and screaming. They were in so much pain. It was awful. I just hugged them and told them that I was so sorry. Then we went back into the house where I immediately began to pray the rosary with them in the living room. This prayer strengthened them and we were able to begin to talk. I stayed with the family for two hours that morning. I could feel the grace of the Holy Spirit within me, the grace of the sacrament of Holy Orders. God strengthened me so that I could strengthen them.

I had to leave around noon, because I had another important event on the schedule. At two o'clock, back at the church, the organ began to play "Pachelbel's Canon" as the bride processed down the aisle. The couple's family and friends had big smiles on their faces and were so joyful. When I saw the bride at the back of the Church, being escorted by her father, I prayed, "Jesus, please give me the grace to be joyful with this family on this day, one of the happiest of their lives." Even though my heart was still heavy for the family who had tragically lost their son, I had to be present with *this* family. Once again, the Holy Spirit gave me the grace I needed. The wedding was beautiful and the new couple left the church for the reception.

That night, as I said my night prayers, I thanked the Lord Jesus that I was a priest. I thanked God that I could bring his grace to families on the worst day of their lives, and on the best day of their lives.

Many of you are probably familiar with the duties of a priest, but others may not be. I knew some seminarians who were converts to the Catholic Faith, so their parents were not Catholic themselves. I also knew some Catholic parents who attended Mass faithfully, but had no idea what the daily life of a priest is really like.

The first and most important part of a priest's role comes directly from Jesus in the Gospel of Matthew, in a passage known as the Great Commission:

> "Then Jesus approached and said to them, 'All power in heaven and on earth has been given to me. Go, therefore, and make disciples of all nations, baptizing them in the name of the Father, and of the Son, and of the Holy Spirit, teaching them to observe all that I have commanded you. And behold, I am with you always, until the end of the age.'"

> Matthew 28:19-20

The overarching mission of a priest is to bring the Gospel, the Good News, to the entire world. The priest is called to do this in the same way as Jesus and his first apostles: by preaching, teaching, and baptizing. But how does this translate into the daily life of the priest?

"The first duty of the priest is to pray," writes St. John Vianney, the patron saint of priests. Every priest makes a promise to pray five times per day for the people of God using a special set of prayers called the Liturgy of the Hours. In addition, priests spend time in private prayer, contemplation, and intercession for all people, especially those who have asked them to pray for them.

The following pages present a thorough (though not exhaustive) list of what a priest does, illustrated with a few stories from my own experience.

1. A priest celebrates Holy Mass each day for the people in his parish. Sunday Mass is the most important because this is when most Catholics are nourished spiritually with the words of Scripture and with the Holy Eucharist, the Body and Blood of Jesus.

2. Spends time praying about the Sunday scripture readings as he prepares his homily for the upcoming Mass. Preparing the Sunday homily can be a very time-consuming part of a priest's life.

3. Works to make sure that the Sunday Masses are as beautiful and well-planned as possible, with sacred

music, well-prepared cantors and choirs, well-trained altar servers, beautiful vestments, beautiful sacred vessels (like chalices), and trained lectors and Eucharistic Ministers. Because this Sunday Mass is so important in the lives of the people, the priest is charged to make it a powerful, uplifting spiritual experience.

4. Teaches classes for young couples to prepare them to have their children baptized. He schedules and celebrates the baptism, often during or after a Sunday Mass.

Sometimes, though, priests are called to celebrate the sacraments at unexpected times, in unexpected ways. I remember a time when I had just celebrated daily Mass and was greeting the people as they came out of the church. An African-American woman whom I did not know walked out and said, "Father, will you come to the hospital and baptize my two little nieces, Sasha and Sabrina? They are twins. They were born pre-maturely last night and are not expected to survive. The mother is my sister and she is Catholic. She asked me to bring you." I went straight to the hospital and made my way to the neo-natal intensive care unit. When I arrived, a young woman was sitting by the two incubators waiting. I had never seen this woman before. She said, "Father, I am not married but I just had these two babies and I want them to be baptized Catholics. Will you do this for me?" Quickly, I asked the young woman to make her profession of faith. I started: "Do you believe in God the Father Almighty, the maker of heaven and earth?" To each question, she replied, "I do." Then, using a medicine dropper and three drops of sterile water, I said, "Sasha, I baptize you in the name of the Father and of the Son and of the Holy Spirit." After both Sasha and Sabrina were baptized, I chatted with the mother for a few minutes and took down the information for the baptism register. I never saw that young African-American mother again, but the nurse called me later that day to tell me that both Sasha and Sabrina had died. These two little girls are in heaven right now with Jesus, and I had something to do with it... because I am a priest.

5. A priest schedules appointments in his office to counsel people regarding their spiritual lives, issues in their families or marriages, problems with their children, etc.

6. Meets with young couples to prepare them for Holy Marriage. This requires several sessions with the couple. The priest schedules and celebrates the Sacrament of Marriage for this couple and their families and friends.

7. Visits the parish school and the Religious Education program so as to teach the children about Jesus Christ and his Church.

8. Teaches Bible studies and catechism classes to help people know their faith better and to practice it more devoutly.

9. Oversees the religious education of children and adults in his parish. This includes the program preparing children to receive the Sacraments of First Communion, First Confession, and Confirmation. The priest plans out these events with his staff and presides over them. (The bishop ordinarily presides over and administers the Sacrament of Confirmation.)

10. Cares for the poor, both within his parish and in the general community, and teaches the people of the parish to do likewise. Most parishes have a social outreach apostolate, such as a St. Vincent de Paul Society, which provides food, housing, clothing and emergency relief to God's beloved poor.

11. Visits people who are in prison to hear their confessions, celebrate Mass, and teach them about scripture and Church teaching.

12. Hears confessions each week at established times in the church and by private appointments in his office.

As a newly ordained priest, I would hear the confessions of our Catholic school children every Friday at the school. No one was forced to come, but I taught the children about the sacrament, and many did come every Friday. I would almost always give these children the same penance. I would say, "Now after school today, I want you to throw your book bag in your mom's car. And then I want you to go into the church for just a minute or two, and kneel down right in front of the Blessed Sacrament, where Jesus is present in the tabernacle. And I want you to say to Jesus, not with your lips but with your heart: 'Jesus, I love you.' And then go back and get into your mom's car." The children loved this penance, and as the school year went on, they would say, "I know my penance, Father!" And I would say, "Yes, go visit Jesus in the church." Before the school bell rang at three o'clock, I would go sit in the balcony of the church, behind the organ where I could not be seen, and I would watch. I would see all of these small children run into the church, genuflect as only a third grader can do, and then kneel right in front of the Blessed Sacrament with their hands folded in prayer. Then they would jump up, make the Sign of the Cross and hurry back to their car. As I sat in that balcony watching, I thanked God that I was a priest. This is how I developed one of the principles that I use daily as a Catholic priest: "Bring people to Jesus and get out of the way!"

13. A priest oversees the Rite of Christian Initiation for Adults (R.C.I.A), which prepares people to join the Catholic Church. The priest teaches quite a few of these classes himself.

14. Teaches people how to pray well and offers opportunities to practice the different methods of prayer. He leads Adoration of the Blessed Sacrament and Benediction, sometimes organizing a Perpetual Adoration Chapel in the parish. He will provide opportunities to pray the Liturgy of the Hours, the rosary, the Chaplet of Divine Mercy, etc.

15. Meets regularly with his parish staff to plan events in the parish that will spiritually nourish and care for the people.

16. Meets regularly with his parish council and finance committee, and gives a pastor's report on the state of the parish, financial and otherwise. He seeks out and considers the advice of these important councils.

17. A priest who is a pastor administers the parish in accord with the directives of the diocesan bishop. The priest

must construct a parish budget, hire employees, make decisions about the upkeep of the physical plant, pay the bills, etc. Normally the parish has a bookkeeper, but the priest must approve all expenditures and sign the checks. He is the pastor with overall jurisdiction for the parish and its people. He is the "Spiritual Father" of this parish family.

18. Attends (at least drops by) many other parish events and meetings. Examples include the Legion of Mary, the Charismatic Prayer Group, the Council of Catholic Women, the Knights of Columbus, the Youth Group, the football and basketball games of the school children, etc. He will also be invited to attend important events in the lives of his parishioners, such as marriage anniversary celebrations, graduations, baptism parties, and other events.

19. A priest goes to hospitals and nursing homes to visit sick parishioners, bringing them Holy Communion and praying with them. He often gives them the healing sacrament called the Anointing of the Sick.

20. Visits sick people in their homes who are not able to come to Mass and brings them these same sacraments.

21. Visits the family when a loved one dies to pray with them and console them. With the family, he will plan and celebrate the funeral Mass, and then go to the cemetery for the final rites of blessing the grave before the burial.

In summary, a priest is charged with preparing the people in his parish to meet Jesus Christ face to face. The priest is a *curate*, a doctor of souls. He heals and strengthens the soul, preparing people for eternal life in heaven.

What about the millions of people who do not know Jesus — both the people across the world, and those across the street from the church? Yes, the mission of the Catholic Church is to evangelize every person, to bring the Good News of Jesus to every person who has not yet received it. These people are also of great concern to every priest, in addition to his own local flock. As my moral theology professor always reminded us in the seminary: "Remember men: you are responsible only for those for whom Jesus Christ died." Of course, Jesus died for all!

Are you surprised that a parish priest has so many duties? How would one priest be able to accomplish all of this? True, some parishes are larger than others, and thus much busier. Some parishes have assistant priests and a large staff to assist the pastor in these different duties.

Some priests are better than others at different aspects of their vocations, which is true of every person in every vocation. Some priests are better preachers and some are better teachers. Some are great administrators and fundraisers. Some have a special gift with the poor. Some are true mystics, with a deep spiritual life, which inspires the people to strive for holiness.

To be a priest is a big job with big responsibilities! If he is doing his job well, the calendar of a priest is usually completely filled. This is why a priest must begin every day with prayer.

"The faithful expect only one thing from priests: that they be specialists in promoting the encounter between man and God. The priest is not asked to be an expert in economics, construction or politics. He is expected to be an expert in the spiritual life."

Pope Benedict XVI

A Priest is Well-Occupied

A priest friend told me once that he was approached by the permanent deacon in his parish, a saintly man, married with several children. The permanent deacon said something which surprised the priest: "Father, will all due respect, I don't think I would ever encourage one of my sons to be a priest." The priest was surprised and responded, "Why would you say that?" The deacon said, "Well, you always seem so rushed and busy, charging from one appointment or event to another. And you always talk about how busy you are. It is hard to imagine my sons happy in that kind of life."

The priest told me that from that day on, he never again used the word "busy." "The truth is," he said, "I am a very happy priest. I love being a priest and I could never do anything else that would fulfill me in the same way. I would choose this life again every day if it were necessary."

He said that from that day on, whenever a parishioner came to him and began with, "Father, I know you are busy but could you...?" he would reply, "Yes, I *am* very well-occupied doing my job, which is to take care of God's beloved children. And *you* are one of those beloved children. So what can I do for you today?"

If your son becomes a priest, this is what he will be doing.

Parents, Priests, and Providence
St. Monica, Mother of St. Augustine

St. Monica was a fourth-century Christian who was given in marriage by her family to a pagan, Patricius, who lived in her hometown of Tagaste in North Africa. Patricius was licentious and had a violent temper. Monica also had to endure a difficult mother-in-law who lived in her home. Patricius criticized his wife because of her goodness and prayerfulness, but he also respected her for her faith. Monica's prayers and example eventually won her husband and mother-in-law to Christianity.

Monica had at least three children but the most famous was Augustine. He was very bright and inquisitive about the faith, but he was also living an immoral life. Augustine had a mistress and eventually an illegitimate son. For a while, Monica refused to let Augustine even eat or sleep in her house. Then one night she had a vision that assured her that her son Augustine would one day be a great Christian. From that time on, she stayed close to him, praying and fasting for him. In fact, she stayed much closer than Augustine wanted!

When he was twenty-nine years old, Augustine went to Rome to study and then to Milan where he came under the influence of the bishop St. Ambrose. His mother followed him, much to his distress! St. Ambrose also became Monica's spiritual director.

A story is told that Monica complained to Ambrose, "I keep trying to talk to my son about God but he will not listen." The wise bishop replied, "Monica, Monica, stop trying to talk to your son about God, and start talking to God about your son."

She continued her prayers and fasting for Augustine until he was baptized a Christian on Easter in the year 387. He eventually became a priest and then bishop of Hippo.

St. Augustine was a philosophical and theological genius. His teaching dominated all of Catholic philosophy and theology for nearly eight hundred years! He is a canonized saint and a giant of the Catholic faith—all because of the prayers and patience of his devoted mother.

CHAPTER 4

LEFT MENDING THE NETS

Four hundred years before Christ, there lived a philosopher named Diogenes of Sinope. One day, Diogenes, who believed in living a very simple life, was sitting in the dirt by the side of the road, eating a bowl of cold gruel. One of his rich childhood friends rode up on a white horse. He was clothed in rich, elegant robes and had silver chains around his neck. He looked down at Diogenes with disgust. He said, "Diogenes, if only you would learn to flatter the king, you would not have to eat that gruel." But Diogenes looked up from the dirt and said, "Oh, but you have it all wrong. If only you would learn to eat this gruel, you would not have to flatter the king."

Having a good perspective is an important part of being a Christian. Your perspective—how you see things—is very important with regard to your son considering priesthood. In this chapter, I would like to help you navigate your own response, emotional and otherwise, to your son's interest in priesthood. How should you feel? What should your position be? You can expect some mood swings, especially when people begin to talk about your son becoming a priest.

Let's be realistic. Family members may feel very differently about a loved one entering seminary, which can cause tension in the family. This is especially true if the man's own mother and father feel very differently about it.

> "Do not think that I have come to bring peace upon the earth. I have come to bring not peace but the sword. For I have come to set a man against his father, a daughter against her mother, and a daughter-in-law against her mother-in-law; and one's enemies will be those of his household. Whoever loves father or mother more than me is not worthy of me, and whoever loves son or daughter more than me is not worthy of me; and whoever does not take up his cross and follow after me is not worthy of me. Whoever finds his life will lose it, and whoever loses his life for my sake will find it."
>
> Mt 10:34-39

31

This is one of those Gospel passages that makes people uncomfortable, but it is true. Jesus knew that family members would disagree with their children's decisions to follow him in a radical way. Let's look at two historical precedents.

The Mother & Brothers of St. Thomas Aquinas

St. Thomas Aquinas was born in 1225 to wealthy and well-educated parents. Most of Thomas's brothers chose military careers, but his mother, a powerful countess, desired for him to become a Benedictine monk. Instead of joining the Benedictines, he wanted to join the Dominican order, a much more humble, simple life. On his way to Rome, Thomas's mother sent her other sons to kidnap him. They took him back to their parents' castle and held him there as a prisoner for two years! His mother was hoping that the detention would mute his aspirations and he would do what she desired.

On one occasion, his brothers became desperate and sent a prostitute into his room to try to seduce Thomas, hoping this would make him forget about priesthood. The story goes that he chased her out with a burning stick from the fire, sending a strong message to his family that he believed completely that God was calling him to become a Dominican priest!

Finally, his family relented. Thomas joined the Dominican order and went on to become a saint and doctor of the Church. His writings have profoundly influenced every area of Catholic philosophy and theology to the present day.

Yes, Jesus knew that there would be problems when he called young people to follow him in a radical way. St. Thomas Aquinas and many other saints came to the point where they realized that their Heavenly Father had more essential things to say to them than their earthly father (or mother). Saints, and all of those called by God to do radical things for the Kingdom, are often misunderstood by their parents and family members, and this causes suffering for both. The call of God is a powerful thing, and parents must be very careful how they respond to it in the lives of their children.

The Father of St. Francis of Assisi

St. Francis of Assisi was born in 1181, also to wealthy parents. His father was a successful cloth merchant and wanted his son to follow in his footsteps. Francis grew up with every opportunity for education and fine things, and he wanted the glory of a soldier. He loved to sing and party with his friends.

His conversion was occasioned by meeting a leper in the countryside. In a moment of grace, Francis jumped from his horse and embraced and kissed the leper, the stench notwithstanding. Francis was filled with joy! As he rode away, he turned to look back and wave, but the leper had disappeared.

Francis began to have conflicts with his father when he made the decision to give clothing to the poor from his family's business, without permission! His father dragged him before the bishop so he would be told to return the cloth and the money. The bishop could see there was something very special about this young man. He did tell Francis to return the money and to trust that "God would provide." St. Francis then left home with nothing, and lived his life as a wandering beggar, serving the poor and preaching the Gospel.

What parent would support his child in a decision like this? How could his parents have known that this bizarre behavior was truly the call of God, and that their son would become one of the most famous saints in the Church? The Franciscans, the order that St. Francis founded, has been joined by thousands of men and women. They have transformed the world through their care for the poor, their missionary endeavors, and their preaching and teaching.

The Opposite Problem: Parental Pressure to Become a Priest

Some parents are *too* excited that their son wants to be a priest. Some men have gone to seminary primarily because they wanted to please their devout mothers. Other men went to seminary, discerned God telling them to leave seminary, but they did not leave because they feared disappointing their families. This is a grave error. When a man is ordained a priest for the wrong reasons, it ends badly.

If God shows a seminarian that he is not called to become a priest, he needs to listen to God and leave the seminary. He should go home and find his true vocation, whether his parents will be happy or sad. I have known many seminarians who discerned out of seminary and returned home to marry, raise families, and do great things for the Church. St. Thomas More is one of the most famous examples of this. He left the Carthusian monastery after trying it for a year or so. He subsequently married, had four children and then became the Chancellor of all England under King Henry VIII. He was eventually martyred because of his fidelity to the Catholic Faith. God has an important plan for all of his children.

A Strange Encounter

I did not go to seminary until after attending a secular college. But in my senior year of high school I was considering priesthood, a fact I did not want known because I was still dating and discerning my vocation. But the news had leaked out to my classmates that I might become a priest, and I was beginning to get comments. One day, one of my classmates, whom I did not know very well, approached me to ask if the rumor was true. I admitted that it was a possibility. He became very upset and practically shouted his objections: "Why would you do this? Have you lost your mind? You don't want a wife? You don't want to have sex?"

I will never forget this scene, as it struck me as very strange. It was certainly inappropriate on his part. So I asked him some questions: "Why are you so upset? Why do *you* care? It's not your life. Why does this bother you so much?"

He realized that he was out of line and calmed down. He mumbled something to the effect of, "Well, I just want you to be happy and not throw away your life. Do what you want." And he walked away.

Later, as I prayed about that encounter, it occurred to me why he may have been upset. He was eighteen years old, just like I was. And he saw that I was contemplating something very serious — the reality of God and the truth that we are on earth to do something meaningful. Perhaps it was threatening to him because he had not contemplated that reality himself?

Secularism: a plan of life that takes no account of where I came from and no account of where I am going.

We live in a secular society, so living and thinking as God does will often be very threatening to others. A Christian lives his life concentrating on the things that last; not on the things that pass. Like my classmate, I think that parents of would-be seminarians can feel challenged by their son's decision. They may think: "I brought this child into the world and raised him, and now he is considering spiritual realities far more seriously than I did at his age." I wonder if this is why some parents become so disconcerted when they hear the news of their son's interest in priesthood? Perhaps it is unsettling to be spiritually challenged by one's own child.

The Gamaliel Principle

The "Gamaliel Principle" is my term for a spiritual "wait and see" approach. It is one of the most consoling concepts for a parent who believes his or her son is making a mistake by pursuing priesthood. This principle comes from the Acts of the Apostles:

> "When they had brought them [the apostles] in and made them stand before the Sanhedrin, the high priest questioned them, 'We gave you strict orders (did we not?) to stop teaching in that name (the name of Jesus). Yet you have filled Jerusalem with your teaching and want to bring this man's blood upon us.' But Peter and the apostles said in reply, 'We must obey God rather than men. The God of our ancestors raised Jesus, though you had him killed by hanging him on a tree. God exalted him at his right hand as leader and savior to grant Israel repentance and forgiveness of sins. We are witnesses of these things, as is the Holy Spirit that God has given to those who obey him.' When they heard this, they became infuriated and wanted to put them to death.

> "But a Pharisee in the Sanhedrin named Gamaliel, a teacher of the law, respected by all the people, stood up, ordered the men to be put outside for a short time, and said to them, 'Fellow Israelites, be careful what you are about to do to these men. Some time ago, Theudas appeared, claiming to be someone important, and about four hundred men joined him, but he was killed, and all those who were loyal to him were disbanded and came to nothing. After him came Judas the Galilean at the time of the census. He also drew people after him, but he too perished and all who were loyal to him were

scattered. So now I tell you, have nothing to do with these men, and let them go. *For if this endeavor or this activity is of human origin, it will destroy itself. But if it comes from God, you will not be able to stop it; you may even find yourselves fighting against God.'*

"They were persuaded by him. After recalling the apostles, they had them flogged, ordered them to stop speaking in the name of Jesus, and dismissed them. So they left the presence of the Sanhedrin, rejoicing that they had been found worthy to suffer dishonor for the sake of the name."

Acts 5:27-41

The Gamaliel Principle states that following Jesus in a radical way, like in priesthood, can most often happen only if God himself is behind it. "For if this endeavor or this activity is of human origin, it will destroy itself. But if it comes from God, you will not be able to stop it; you may even find yourselves fighting against God."

The authentic call of God is too powerful for anyone to try to stop, even if parents are very sincerely trying to protect their children, which is their God-given duty.

Let's be clear, though: the call your son feels may *not* be authentic. If you suspect this to be true, your job as a parent is to encourage your son to make a *diligent discernment,* which is described in Chapters 2 and 6.

If he desires to be a priest, let him contact the Vocation Director and begin the application process for seminary. Perhaps God wants him in seminary for a short time and then he will be called out of seminary to his true vocation. If priesthood is something that he wants for himself, or if he wants it for the wrong reasons, it will not endure. But if this is the authentic call of God for his life, he *will* be able to make it through seminary and be ordained a priest. God will give him the grace. And as a parent or family member, you do not want to stop it. God loves your son even more than you do, and knows with all certainty what will make him happy and fulfilled!

> *"Really wanting what God wants is the only way you can know peace in every experience that comes your way."*

St. Therese of Lisieux

Zebedee, Then and Now

In the Introduction, I quoted the gospel passage about Zebedee, the father of James and John. I have always felt compassion for poor Zebedee, even as I feel compassion for parents who are struggling with the vocation of their son. When Jesus called, Zebedee's sons left their father alone in the boat mending the nets. Can you imagine the conversation Zebedee had with his wife that night at dinner? I imagine they were not a happy couple.

Today, though, Zebedee and his wife are rejoicing in Heaven that Jesus came walking by that day two thousand years ago. They are rejoicing that their sons were chosen by the Lord Jesus to be his apostles. Zebedee, right now, is very happy that Christ called his sons, Saint James and Saint John, to be priests. And this will be his sentiment for all eternity.

Praying for a Priest in the Family

Raising her family in the mid-1800s in England, Mrs. Vaughn made a daily holy hour before the Blessed Sacrament for twenty years, praying that she might give all of her children to God.

God answered her prayers! Of her thirteen children, her five daughters entered the convent and six of her eight sons became priests. Of these, three became bishops. One was auxiliary bishop of Salford; another was archbishop of Sydney, Australia; the third and eldest was the great Cardinal, Archbishop of Westminster, builder of Westminster Cathedral and founder of two religious congregations, Herbert Vaughn. The congregations he founded were The Mill Hill Fathers and Sisters. The latter flourished as a Franciscan Sisterhood in Baltimore. The eleven vocations cost, roughly, 7,300 hours of prayer!

Cardinal Vaughn declared that he owed his vocation to the priesthood to his mother's prayers before the Blessed Sacrament and at Communion. At the age of twenty-one, he wrote: "During the day my mother often prayed before the Blessed Sacrament. Every morning before breakfast, she was in the chapel for half an hour or three quarters of an hour. After breakfast, an hour in the morning was always spent in meditation in the chapel, which was her real home. I do not remember ever seeing her look anywhere except at the Blessed Sacrament or into her book during these visits. Even in those days, I was struck with my sweet mother's ardent devotion and love for the Blessed Sacrament."[4]

resentment has become larger. It feels like tearing the scab off of an old wound."

Why would parents be opposed — or at least hesitant — about their son becoming a priest? Here are some common reasons.

1. I am concerned that my son will be unhappy as a priest.

Let me admit that some priests are clearly unhappy. Some priests display their discontent by how they carry themselves and how they treat others. After the Second Vatican Council, there were quite a few defections from the priesthood, which is an obvious indication of unhappiness. If, as a parent, you knew an unhappy priest, it is understandable why you would worry about your son following in his footsteps. Nonetheless, these priests are a very small percentage of the whole, and my sense is that they are becoming increasingly rare. As I showed in Chapter 2, more than ninety percent of priests report being happy and fulfilled.

In my experience, when parents worry that their son will not be happy as a priest, they usually are inferring that he would be happier in marriage. The statistics do not support that assertion. Half of marriages end in divorce, and many of those who remain married report dissatisfaction in their marriages. Thus the statistical chances for happiness and fulfillment are actually much better in priesthood. The vast majority of priests are happy and say they would choose priesthood again.

Why are priests so happy? Because they are committed to a mission of eternal consequence. Many years ago I read the results of a survey of high school and college students. One question asked, "Why would a man want to become a priest?" The most common answer was: "To do something that matters. To do something that will change the world."

Priests are doing something that will give people ultimate fulfillment and happiness. This is why priests are often well-respected even by non-Catholics. All people can see that priests are doing something extraordinarily meaningful. Living one's life in this way gives a person great purpose and personal happiness. Perhaps you have heard the expression: "Priesthood: The pay isn't great but the retirement benefits are out of this world!"

Msgr. Stephen Rossetti, in his book *Why Priests are Happy*, presents solid data from his research about how priests view their lives and ministry. He was interviewed by Zenit, a Catholic news service, about this study. In the interview, Msgr. Rossetti cites his own research showing that the majority of priests are happy and fulfilled. In addition, he cites other studies by secular researchers that consistently show that clergy in general are the happiest of all Americans. He said:

"But this consistent and astounding finding of priestly happiness remains a secret. Why? First of all, good news doesn't make the news. Tragedies and scandals fill our front pages but the faces of our many happy priests do not. Second, and just as important, the secularization of our culture breeds a kind of negativism toward organized religion. There is a secular belief among some today that practicing the faith must be constraining and joyless. Some modern thinkers suggest that the only way to true human happiness is to be freed from the constraints of religion. They see religion as repressive of one's true human freedom and humanity. Thus, using this logic, being a priest must be the unhappiest life of all.

"Therefore, to hear that priests are among the happiest people in the country is met with disbelief. The fact of priestly happiness is a fundamental and powerful challenge to the modern secular mind. But for us Christians, it only confirms the truths of our faith. Jesus prayed, "That my joy might be yours, and your joy might be complete." Joy is one of the unmistakable fruits of the Holy Spirit. To be truly and fully Christian is to know God's gift of joy. The secular mind searches for this joy, but it is looking in the wrong place. It only makes sense that those men who have dedicated their lives in the service of God and others in the Catholic faith as priests would be slowly and gently filled by God with an inner happiness and joy. Jesus promised us his joy and it is demonstrably true....

leaving the priesthood. Given the enormous pressure on priesthood today and the many real challenges facing these men, this is remarkable.

"This is the real truth underlying the findings of the study: Our priests are happy and holy men."[5]

2. I don't understand why priests have to be celibate.

I once heard the story of the Lotha tribe in Nagaland, India, a place that many Protestant missionaries had visited. They had all tried to convert the tribesmen to Christianity, but no one could convince the elderly chief to convert, and his decision was determinative for the others. Finally, in 1952, a Catholic priest went to this tribe and began to preach the Christian message, much as the Protestant missionaries had done before him. When the chief, Mothungo Ezung, learned that the priest was celibate — not married precisely to show the world that the Christian message about eternal life is true — he converted to the Catholic Faith immediately, taking the baptismal name Peter. The chief was impressed and inspired that priests were willing to forgo something as valuable as marriage and children, because of Jesus Christ and his promise of eternal life. With the chief, 2,600 people in four villages converted to Christianity! At the time of this writing, the chief's grandson, Mhonchan Ezung, is a seminarian for the diocese of Metuchen, New Jersey.

"In an age so steeped in sex and pleasure-seeking materialism, should there not be somewhere on this planet those who joyously and generously offer their bodies as concrete proof of their conviction of the supremacy of the spiritual over the material, and as a sign of love for Him who did not spare even His own Son for love of us?"

Jean Guitton, French Philosopher

The requirement of celibacy is one of the greatest sources of anxiety for a man who is discerning priesthood, so it is understandable why parents also would worry. We live in a sex-saturated society. Sex or sensuality is featured on our televisions, computers, billboards, and magazines. The message we receive from the media is very clear: no person can be happy and fulfilled unless they are having a lot of sex. This is simply not true. But if you speak a lie often enough, people begin to believe it. This is one of the reasons many people are skeptical about celibacy.

In the Latin Church, it is understood that when God calls a man to the priesthood, he is also calling him to apostolic celibacy — the state of being unmarried and thus abstaining from sexual relations for the sake of the Kingdom of Heaven. Why is this? A veritable library of books has been written on the subject, and I cannot hope to present the rich history of celibacy in a few pages. So let me present five key concepts to help you understand celibacy from the Church's point of view.

First, celibacy does not imply that sexual relations in marriage are impure — to the contrary! The Church has always upheld the beauty of marriage and family, often in spite of intense pressure by societies or governments to weaken or "broaden" this sacred institution. A respect for marriage goes hand-in-hand with respect for celibacy:

> "Most Catholic people marry, and all Catholics are taught to venerate marriage as a holy institution — a sacrament, an action of God upon our souls; one of the holiest things we encounter in this life. In fact, it is precisely the holiness of marriage that makes celibacy precious; for only what is good and holy in itself can be given up for God as a sacrifice. Just as fasting presupposes the goodness of food, celibacy presupposes the goodness of marriage. To despise celibacy, therefore, is to undermine marriage itself — as the early Fathers pointed out."[6]

Second, instead of committing to a single woman, a priest gives himself to every man, woman, and child. This is the practical aspect of celibacy. A priest does not go to work, earn a living, and return home to the demands of ordinary family life. Instead, he sacrifices the good of wife and children in order to be free to serve the parish. He is up early, not to feed his children breakfast, but to feed the people of God with the Eucharist. He is up late, not to pore over finances with his wife, but to review the

Third, celibacy is firmly rooted in scripture and Church tradition. Jesus himself said that some people "have renounced marriage for the sake of the kingdom of God. Whoever can accept this ought to accept it" (Mt 19:12). Writing a few years after Jesus' resurrection, St. Paul also recommended celibacy, saying, "The unmarried man is anxious about the affairs of the Lord, how to please the Lord; but the married man is anxious about worldly affairs, how to please his wife, and his interests are divided" (1 Cor 7:27-34). This preference for priestly celibacy persisted in the early Church and quickly became the norm.

Fourth, Jesus was celibate. Jesus never married because that was not the plan of the Father for him. A priest is asked to be like Jesus as much as possible, and to imitate Jesus by giving himself completely as a gift to others. To understand this, we need to refer to a key theological concept found in scripture: throughout the New Testament, Jesus is described as the bridegroom and the Church as the bride. Now, because we understand that a priest is functioning *in persona Christi capitis* (in the person of Christ, the head of the Church), we can see that the priest symbolizes Christ's union with the Church. At no time is this clearer than when a priest celebrates Holy Mass. As the priest stands at the altar, saying, "This is my Body, given up for you," in essence he is renewing Jesus' wedding vows to the Church. In this sense, the Mass is a profound act of marital intimacy. The priest's celibacy mirrors Jesus' celibacy, his exclusive love for his bride, the Church.

Fifth, and perhaps most important, celibacy reminds us of the reality of heaven. Jesus taught that there is no marriage in heaven between men and women (Mark 12:25). This is because heaven *is* a wedding feast — the eternal celebration of the union between Jesus and his bride, the Church. This heavenly marriage is the *real* marriage, the one that lasts forever.

> "For this reason a man shall leave his father and mother and shall be joined to his wife, and the two shall become one flesh. *This mystery is great; but I am speaking with reference to Christ and the church.* Nevertheless, each individual among you also is to love his own wife even as himself, and the wife must see to it that she respects her husband."
>
> Ephesians 5: 31-33

I certainly realize that these are profound concepts, especially if you are considering them for the first time. You may be wondering how a man could forgo sex his whole life based on some metaphors from scripture. But these are no ordinary metaphors. To explain, I'm going to appeal to one of the most famous philosophical texts of all time, Plato's *Allegory of the Cave*.

The ancient philosopher Plato describes a cave in which people have lived their whole lives, chained facing the back wall. They see shadows on the wall caused by light entering from the mouth of the cave and they believe the shadows are real life because they cannot leave the cave or even turn around and see the light. When one person escapes the cave, he discovers the shadows are actually caused by real objects which he can now see in the light of the sun. He returns to the cave, but he cannot convince the others who remain in the cave of the truth of his discovery. The point is that there are eternal realities that are more profound and more real than earthly realities. Plato understood this, long before Christian revelation. But this is difficult for most people to accept.

Let's apply the Allegory of the Cave to marriage. In a sense, marriage is like a "shadow" of a more fundamental reality: heaven. In heaven, we will be united to God and each other for ever, in a union far deeper than the most sensual marital embrace. That is why in scripture, God uses the analogy of marriage, a reality we can understand, to help us imagine heaven, which is more difficult to understand. Thus celibacy — an absurdity to the world — is a radical sign that *heaven is real*. When a priest gives up marriage and responds to a call to celibacy, people know he's serious about the things above. He's willing to make a tremendous sacrifice on earth to help people look toward the reality of heaven.

Pope St. John Paul II, in his ground breaking work, *The Theology of the Body,* spends a great deal of time on this subject. To paraphrase, he says that all analogies are inadequate to describe our union with God in Heaven. But of all analogies, the marital embrace is the least inadequate.

Even the infamous atheist philosopher Friedrich Nietzsche, certainly no friend of the Catholic Church, recognized the value of celibacy. He observed that celibacy signifies to the laity that the

"Martin Luther gave back to the priest sexual intercourse with women; but three quarters of the reverence of which the common people, especially the women among the common people, are capable, rests on the faith that a person who is an exception at this point will be an exception in other respects as well... Luther, having given woman to the priest, had to take away from him auricular confession; that was right psychologically. With that development the Christian priesthood was fundamentally abolished, because his most profound utility had always been that he was a holy ear, a silent well, a grave for secrets."[7]

Sometimes married couples themselves have a profound understanding of celibacy because of their life circumstances. I knew of a seminarian who was approaching his diaconate ordination, the time when he would have to make his life-long promise of celibacy. He was very nervous. Though he had prayed long and hard, he was still not sure if he would be able to make this promise in tranquility of heart. Several times, he had mentioned his concerns to his father, a devout Catholic man and a wonderful father. Each time, his father had counseled him, "Well, just continue to pray about it and Jesus will guide you. He will give you the grace you need to do what He asks of you." One day, the two were riding in a car together and the seminarian once again expressed his concern about celibacy, and the father replied with the same, solid advice. This time, the seminarian became angry and shouted at his dad, "What do you know about celibacy? You are a married man. How can you know what I am dealing with?" The father pulled the car over to the side of the road and he turned it off. He said to his son, "Do you remember many years ago when your mother was in that terrible car accident? The seminarian replied, "Yes, of course. She almost died." The father continued, "Since that time fifteen years ago, because of her injuries and the required medications, your mother and I have not been able to have sexual relations at all." The young man was incredulous. He said, "Dad, I never knew that. I am so sorry. But how did you do it? You were just a young man yourself." The father replied calmly, "I love your mother with a higher love than just the physical and I will love her and stay faithful to her until the day I die. Jesus gives me the grace to do what He asks of me." The young man began to cry. He realized that his father's advice came from a great understanding. Love and suffering are mystically related, and we are all called to that higher love which always involves suffering. Jesus always gives us the grace to do what He asks us to do. The young man was ordained a deacon, and he is a happy priest today.

Let me end this section with a practical illustration of the wisdom of celibacy, again from the perspective of a married man. A good friend of mine is a Methodist minister and a very holy, dedicated servant of God. He once told me this story:

> "I was pastoring a very large church and really exerting myself to take care of so many people. One day, I left my house at six o'clock in the morning. and never stopped the entire day. At around seven thirty that night, my wife called me on my cell phone and asked, 'Are you going to come home and make love to me tonight? Or are you going to stay and make love to your church?' I asked, 'Is it that bad?' She replied, 'Yes.'"

This minister acknowledged that, although he loved his wife and children very much, he also admired and respected the discipline of celibacy in the Catholic priesthood. He understood why Jesus would recommend celibacy for his priests. A priest gives all his love to Jesus and his Church.

"The spiritual children which the Lord gives each priest, the children he has baptized, the families he has blessed and helped on their way, the sick he has comforted, the young people he catechizes and helps to grow, the poor he assists… all these are the 'Bride' whom he rejoices to treat as his supreme and only love and to whom he is constantly faithful."

Pope Francis, Chrism Mass, 2014

---

3. I want my son to have a successful career.

Most parents have aspirations for their son's career. They

was not what I expected. He won't be able to take care of us financially when we are old."

Parents can be disappointed by their children's choice of occupation even if they are not called to priesthood. A young woman who used to come to me for spiritual direction told me that her parents really wanted her to enter the medical profession. So in college she began moving towards physical therapy. Halfway toward obtaining her degree, she discovered she just did not enjoy it and wanted to become a teacher instead. Her parents were not happy. But today this woman is very happy as a second grade teacher in a Catholic school.

There are times when a family has an established, successful business that has sustained them for many years. Fathers and mothers very much want that business to continue, being operated under the family name. My family had a large farming and tobacco warehouse business and my father very much hoped that one of his sons would take it over.

St. Francis of Assisi's father was a successful cloth merchant and would have passed on to Francis the family business. St. Francis walked away from this, ironically, completely naked, and spent his life in full time service of Jesus Christ! St. Francis has been known and loved all over the world since his death in 1226. There are thousands of churches, schools, hospitals, and other Catholic institutions named for St. Francis. His statue adorns gardens in every nation. His life and teachings have inspired millions of people to know and love Jesus better, and this will continue until Jesus comes again. I hardly think St. Francis would have been that "successful" in his father's clothing business.

4. I am afraid that my son will be lonely as a priest.

Loneliness has been part of the human condition ever since original sin. People in every vocation experience loneliness from time to time. The worst loneliness in the world is to be married to a person whom you do not love, or who does not love you. It is very sad for a person to have to sleep in the same bed with another person, their spouse, when there is no tenderness or kindness.

Interestingly, married and single people who come to me for spiritual direction describe loneliness as an issue far more often than priests and religious sisters. Most priests I know do not consider loneliness to be a great problem in their lives because so much of their time is spent with people who love them. Living celibately as a priest does not mean that a priest has no intimacy in his life. On the contrary, most priests would say that they feel the love and support of so many people that it can be humbling and even overwhelming.

There is another reason why most priests and religious do not experience chronic loneliness. It is their life of prayer. It is only when a person spends much time alone with God that he realizes that he is never alone! Because a priest spends silent time every day alone in prayer, he feels a powerful, spiritual connection with Jesus.

If you are worried that your son will be lonely, or not happy and fulfilled, I recommend that you talk with your own parish priest, or with the parents of priests in your diocese. They will reassure you that priests, by and large, are very satisfied in their vocation. I know many priests. And I would say that I know twenty happy priests for every one priest who says he is unhappy or lonely.

5. I feel like I am losing my son.

"Each year his parents went to Jerusalem for the feast of Passover, and when he was twelve years old, they went up according to festival custom. After they had completed its days, as they were returning, the boy Jesus remained behind in Jerusalem, but his parents did not know it. Thinking that he was in the caravan, they journeyed for a day and looked for him among their relatives and acquaintances, but not finding him, they returned to Jerusalem to look for him. After three days they found him in the temple, sitting in the midst of the teachers, listening to them and asking them questions, and all who heard him were astounded at his understanding and his answers. When his parents saw him, they were astonished, and his mother said to him, *'Son, why have you done this to us? Your father and I have been looking for you with great anxiety.' And he said to them, 'Why were you looking for me? Did you not know that I must be in my Father's house?'* But they did not understand advanced in wisdom and age and favor before God and man."

Luke 2:41-52

Mary and Joseph certainly had the fear that they had lost their twelve-year-old son. They searched for Jesus in the crowded streets of Jerusalem for three days, their hearts in anguish. Remember that a young boy became a man at the age of twelve in ancient Judaism, even though we all know that a twelve year old has much to learn. But Jesus was not lost. He was living in the plan of his Father.

I once heard a priest from England tell his vocation story. As a college student, not really practicing his faith, he was once invited to a luxurious formal party at a large mansion. At some point during the party, he found himself standing at the staircase looking up at the portrait of a very beautiful young woman. As he stared, he heard a voice behind him say, "She's very beautiful, isn't she?" Turning around, he found himself speaking with the lady of the mansion. She said, "That is my daughter. I lost her." The young man stammered, "I am so sorry. How did she die?" The woman replied, "Well, she is not actually dead, but she is dead to me. She left last year and moved to Calcutta to join a religious order, the Missionaries of Charity. She had everything here; the love of her family, a superb education, friends, wealth, fun. She gave all of that up and now she lives in a dirty city, praying and taking care of poor, sick, and dying people whom she doesn't even know. I've lost her."

The priest said that he developed a friendship with that woman and he was invited back for meals and socials. While in the home, he found himself often staring at the portrait and wondering about the young woman. Eventually, the mother asked him, "You are such a fine young man. Would you go to Calcutta and try to bring my daughter back?" The young man was enamored with her beauty and saw an opportunity to meet the young woman in person, so he agreed. The family paid all of his expenses and he flew to India. When he arrived, he finally reached the moment for which he had been waiting. He met this young religious sister and interviewed her about her life. He was amazed at how joyful she was, though he could not understand how this could be, as she lived in such poverty. He was amazed that she would give up everything the world considers precious in order to work with the sick and poor.

Finally, even though his heart was burning, he said that he became exasperated with her answers to his questions and he blurted out: "How can you live in this filth, when you had everything?" And the young Missionary of Charity calmly replied: "How can you live in your filth?"

The interview was over. The young man returned to England alone, with the words of this young sister burning in his mind and heart. "How can you live in your filth?" These words continued to burn and they were the impetus for his reversion to Jesus Christ. He began to practice his Catholic faith again, he repented of his sins, went to confession, and he eventually went to the seminary and became a priest.

The mother of the rich young woman in this true story really felt like she had lost her daughter, but as this young man discovered, the daughter had found herself.

"Jesus Christ alone fully reveals man to himself and makes his supreme calling clear."[8]

Pastoral Constitution on the Church in the Modern World

It is only in Jesus Christ that a person can truly know who he is and what he is called to be. This is the essence of a vocation. But I do feel compassion for parents who feel like they have lost their child.

The gift of your son to God was first made many years ago at his baptism. You asked God to adopt him, that he would be a child of the light and call God his Father in the midst of the Church. God accepted your gift and now he has called your son to be a priest. Even if you *feel* that you have lost him, know that you have "lost" him in the most wonderful way. And you will find him in a new and better way.

6. I am not very religious myself.

Some parents are not very religious or their faith practice is minimal. Obviously, this will be a factor in how supportive a parent feels when their son goes to the seminary.

much useless. It seems non-productive and may even be counter-productive. It can be very frustrating."

"For those who believe, no explanation is necessary. For those who do not believe, no explanation is possible."

Franz Werfel

Yes, but it is also very frustrating for the parent. Every person's faith is in a different place. God gives different amounts of faith, hope, and love to different people at different times in their lives. He is the one with the master plan!

I believe that at least one of the reasons God calls some men to priesthood is to strengthen the faith of their parents. One father told his son's vocation director, tongue in cheek: "Father, tell God that I will start coming back to Mass beginning this Sunday; I will even come to confession, if he will just leave my son alone." Even if your faith practice is minimal, there is time to change that.

7. I have had negative experiences with the Church.

Some parents have had a negative encounter with a priest. Some feel uneasy about some particular aspect of Church teaching. Thus it feels like a betrayal when your son wants to dedicate himself to what you might consider to be a tainted or misguided institution.

As one parent said to his son with some anger: "Now that you are going to be a priest, maybe you can help me understand why the Catholic Church teaches that contraception is sinful. I have never understood that teaching!"

Contraception, divorce and remarriage, the homosexual lifestyle, priestly celibacy, the role of women in the Church — all of these make the usual list of grievances. Clearly, if parents do not understand or accept the Church's teachings as true, it will affect how they feel about their son going to the seminary.

Ironically, the father I mentioned above is probably right about his assertion. His son will study all of these teachings in great detail in the seminary and he will likely be able to explain them to his father in a way that will be helpful.

8. I don't want my son to be labeled

The horrible sexual abuse scandal in the Catholic Church will certainly come to mind when your son expresses an interest in priesthood. Even if you recognize the fact that an extremely small percentage of priests were guilty of these crimes, a single case of child sexual abuse by a priest is far too many.

Honest people acknowledge that the sexual abuse of children by adults is a societal problem and not just a problem in the Catholic Church or with priests. Visit any Department of Family and Children Services in any city, and ask them how many cases of child sexual abuse they deal with per month and how many of these terrible crimes were perpetrated by Catholic priests. In most cases, the answer will be many, many cases of sexual abuse and zero perpetrated by priests. Still, the Catholic Church did have this problem and she has addressed it and continues to do so. The cases which make the newspapers regarding priests are almost all cases from thirty to fifty years ago, before our present psychological screening processes.

Today, the screening procedures for prospective seminarians are extremely thorough. Bishops and vocation directors will not accept any candidate who shows even a slight inclination to aberrant sexual behavior toward children. Thus, vocation directors and bishops, if they err, always try to err on the side of the Church. In other words, if there are any doubts that a man is not psycho-sexually healthy, he will not be accepted. Your son, if he applies to the seminary, will be examined very closely in regard to these issues.

Because of the sex abuse scandal, the discipline of celibacy, and a very disordered view of human sexuality in our society, seminarians are sometimes accused of being homosexual, or at least assumed to be. This is an occupational hazard due to our disordered culture. The reality is that the vast majority of priests have a normal heterosexual attraction to women.

The Church is very clear that she desires to ordain normal, healthy men to the priesthood, the same kind of men who would make the best husbands and fathers. These are the men who are capable of being good spiritual fathers for their parish family.

9. I want grandchildren!

Grandchildren are one of the greatest blessings of life. Parents dream about the day when they can love and spoil their grandchildren! There is even a blessing in scripture that speaks of "living to see your children's children" (Psalm 128:6). Understandably, when a parent receives the news that his son wants to go to the seminary, missing out on grandchildren will come to mind.

Most Catholic families in the U.S. today have an average of two children. This differs greatly from the 1950s, for example, when Catholic families had on average at least four children. Parents desire grandchildren, and they are very conscious that if they have only two children, their chances are limited. Many parents mention this as the primary reason they are hesitant about their son going to the seminary.

Priests are called "Father" precisely because of their spiritual fecundity. Priests have many, many spiritual children, because every child of God is the child of God's priest. To look at it in this way, the parents of a priest will have thousands and thousands of spiritual grandchildren. If your son becomes a priest, it is true that no one will call him "daddy," but thousands will call him "Father."

10. I have very little knowledge about seminary or the actual life of a priest.

Many parents today share this sentiment, which is the primary purpose of this book. For this reason, the daily life and duties of a priest were covered in Chapter 3, and seminary life will be addressed in Chapter 8.

Parents, knowledge is power! Talk to priests about their lives, read about priesthood, and learn about life in seminary. Having done so, you will have more peace in this regard.

In spite of these ten most common objections, I hope that you will be able to support your son in his vocation and be positive about priesthood. In general, the more you learn and understand about priesthood and priestly formation, the easier this will be. I always counsel seminarians to be very patient with their families in this regard. I tell them, "This is not easy for your parents! Pray for them and be patient. When they have concerns, talk to them about these things and listen to them with kindness and understanding. But then, do what Jesus tells you, for the will of God is always what is best both for your parents and for you."

"How many parents, after watching their son celebrate sacred Mass, receiving Communion from his hands and a blessing from his lips, could walk out of the church and say they wish he had chosen another profession?"[9]

The mother of Fr. Andrew Wisdom, O.P.

The Father of Pope St. John Paul II

The story is told of the young Karol Wojtyla, the future Pope John Paul II, when he was a small boy. His mother had already died and his brother had left home for his required military service in the Polish army. He and his father lived alone. Every night, the small boy would kneel by his bed to say his prayers while his father stood in the doorway listening.

One night, on hearing the boy pray, the father did not think it was sufficient. So he knelt down beside him and taught him to pray to the Holy Spirit, the well known Catholic prayer that begins "Come Holy Spirit." Pope John Paul II wrote that, from that night, he prayed that prayer every single night throughout his adolescence. He continued to kneel by his bed and say that prayer while he was in the seminary and after he was ordained a priest. He said it daily as a bishop and a cardinal. When elected Pope, he acknowledged that one of the reasons he chose to write an encyclical on the Holy Spirit, *Dominum Et Vivificantem* (On the Holy Spirit in the Life of the Church) was because his father taught him that prayer when he was a child.

Parents, please do not underestimate what you are doing when you teach your children to pray. You never know who and what your children may become!

CHAPTER 6

IS MY SON TOO YOUNG?

- Even if he is truly called to priesthood, at what point should he begin studies?
- Should he go to college first, date, and get a marketable degree?
- Should he go to a college seminary if he feels ready?
- Aren't these very big decisions for a very young man to make?

"It may be hard for an egg to turn into a bird; it would be a jolly sight harder for it to fly while remaining an egg. We are like eggs at present. And you cannot go on indefinitely being just an ordinary, decent egg. We must be hatched or go bad."[10]

C.S. Lewis

If a young man is interested in priesthood, at what point should he go to seminary? At what point is an egg ready to hatch and move forward? I have fielded these questions many times through the years, both from candidates and from their parents. These questions do not have definitive answers because every man is absolutely unique.

Personally, I feel that in today's climate, too many young men are talked out of seminary by well-meaning friends and family. In general, if a man has a desire to pursue priesthood, has done a diligent discernment and displays sufficient maturity, he should give seminary a shot.

In discerning priesthood, I have always taught that there are two very important decisions to make. First, *should* I go to the seminary and give it a try? Second, *when* should I go? Timing is very important. Veteran vocation directors know the truth of this expression: "A vocation is like fruit on the tree; if you pick it too soon, it is not ready. But if it stays on too long, it rots."

The men who counsel your son—his spiritual director, the

sitter." The jumper is a young man who goes away on a retreat, gets excited about priesthood and decides overnight to go to seminary. This is not prudent. He has not completed a diligent discernment. Experience shows that a man like this jumps out of seminary just as quickly as he jumps in.

The fence sitter is the man who never makes a decision to do anything, except to keep discerning and thinking about it. This man could still be discerning and thinking about it when he is sixty years old! The famous axiom *"virtus en medio stat"* applies here: virtue always stands in the middle. The vocation director will want your son to make a good, careful decision after a proper period of sincere prayer and thought. But, when the time comes, he must make a decision! If the fruit stays on too long, it rots.

"Before I formed you in the womb I knew you, before you were born I dedicated you, a prophet to the nations I appointed you. 'Ah, Lord God!' I said, 'I know not how to speak; I am too young.' But the Lord answered me, 'Say not, "I am too young." To whomever I send you, you shall go; whatever I command you, you shall speak. Have no fear before them, because I am with you to deliver you, says the Lord.' Then the Lord extended his hand and touched my mouth, saying, 'See, I place my words in your mouth!'"

Jeremiah 1:5-9

Here are some scenarios, taken from my experience, which illustrate when a young man is ready for seminary and when he is not. Keep in mind, of course, that every situation is unique.

Scenario One: Peter – College Seminary

Peter was only nine years old when he first told his parents that he wanted to be a priest. They smiled and affirmed him for his goodness, but suspected that his inclination would pass. But it did not pass. He mentioned it regularly to his family. Though he never spoke of it at school, his friends called him "Fr. Peter" just because of his demeanor. He was very bright and had a gentle spirit. He was liked by his classmates, but he was not the most popular student, precisely because he was so much more mature than his peers.

Peter's classmates would come to him to talk about their problems and anxieties, especially in middle school and high school. Peter always listened patiently and gave good advice. He rather enjoyed his status of being the class counselor.

He was a faithful altar boy and showed great reverence and respect for the Holy Mass. He was close to the parish priests and they could see he may have a vocation to priesthood, and they invited him to consider it. Peter would always reply that he was praying about it, but that he was not sure yet.

In high school, he branched out a bit more and got involved in various activities, usually taking a leadership role. He was on the Student Council and belonged to the Honor Society. Teachers, parents, and peers respected him. Peter went on a few dates in high school, for the "expected" events like the prom and Valentine's Day dance.

The truth is that Peter could have done most anything with his life. He could have been a psychologist, an engineer, or an architect. He could have run for political office and won.

As Peter's senior year of high school approached, his parents began to question him about his college plans. His SAT scores would have gotten him into most any college he chose. They knew that he had been going to spiritual direction with his local priest for two years and that he still was considering priesthood. His parents thought priesthood would be explored after college, so they were surprised when their son asked their permission to attend a college seminary. As expected, he had done all the research and had satisfactory answers to all their questions. He had been speaking with the vocation director, and the vocation director could clearly see that this man was a great candidate for college seminary. His parents agreed, and gave their permission, even though they would have preferred that he attend ordinary college a year or two first.

Scenario 2: Michael – College Before Seminary

Michael was a good kid and people always commented that he was "all boy." He had all the interests of an ordinary boy and loved sports, movies, video games, and playing with his friends. He was an average boy in many ways, but also above average in friends. He was not the best athlete in his class, but he was in the top half, just above average. He was not the smartest in his class, but he did well in school. At his Catholic school, he listened and learned about Jesus and the Catholic faith, and he showed as much interest as the other children, perhaps a bit more.

But Michael did not mature quite as quickly as his parents would have preferred. In middle school and even into high school, he made some imprudent choices and found himself getting into trouble. He was always sincerely sorry. He would ask forgiveness from his parents and he would even go to confession. He had a good heart, but he was just not very focused. Though he went to Mass without complaining, he was not able to maintain a consistent prayer life. His faith came in fits and bursts; it was not regular.

By high school, Michael's parents recognized a worrisome pattern. He would become very interested in something, almost to the point of obsession, for several months at a time. Then suddenly he would lose interest and drop it completely. In middle school, it was soccer. Then in ninth grade, he dropped the sport, discovering that he was only an average soccer player at the varsity level. He then got very involved in the drama club, but dropped that completely within a year. This pattern continued with other activities. Though his parents wanted him to experience these different things, to find his gifts, they could also see that he needed more perseverance.

During his senior year, Michael went on a retreat with his youth group and he had a powerful spiritual experience. The young priest who was the retreat master impressed and inspired Michael very much! He spoke of how much he loved being a priest and told stories of his life. Michael became enamored of priesthood and he started going to daily Mass and reading spiritual books. When he discovered that the application deadline for applying to the diocese was near, he started talking about going to the seminary after graduation. His parents discouraged him and he got very angry with them. They argued that he did not have the maturity nor the stability to make a decision about his vocation. The three of them went to speak with the vocation director. He listened carefully and asked many questions. He admired Peter's goodness and generosity, but he also recommended that he listen to his parents at this time. He said, "Peter, you may truly have a vocation to be a priest, but I want you to go to college first and stay in touch with me. I want you to mature and to grow in Christian virtue a bit more before you begin seminary."

Scenario 3: Micah – Pursuing Priesthood for Wrong Reasons

Micah was always a sensitive boy, even when he was very small. He would cry when his parents simply raised their voices to correct his behavior. He sincerely tried to be good. He wanted to please his parents, and this desire to "please" carried over into faith life and his schoolwork. He was not a great student and he suffered when he made poor grades, especially when he knew he had not done his best. He was hard on himself. His parents hired tutors to help him in middle school.

Micah never really mentioned an interest in priesthood growing up, though he was personally invited to consider it by the bishop at his Confirmation. Micah told his parents later on that he did not feel called to be a priest. A serious boy, he seemed more mature than his peers and was dutiful in his devotional life. He went to Mass faithfully and said his prayers every night. His parents were very religious and they still prayed and hoped that he might eventually be called. They told him more than once that they would support him if he were called to become a priest.

In his junior year of high school, Micah got a girlfriend, his first ever, and he fell very hard. He was on the phone with her every night and spent far too much time in the relationship. His grades began to drop quickly. Though they were trying not to go "too far," the relationship got more and more physical and eventually, they had intercourse. Micah was devastated and for several weeks, he lived in terror that his girlfriend had become pregnant. He had a very sensitive moral conscience and punished himself severely for this fall. He asked her forgiveness and went to confession, but he did not forgive himself. He broke up with his girlfriend and began to isolate himself. He would not dare tell his parents what had happened and he began to spend a lot more time in church.

As his senior year began, Micah went to his parents to tell them that he wanted to go to the seminary. They were surprised and hesitant. He reminded them that they had promised to support him if he decided to become a priest. They said that they would, but they were worried as his behavior was not quite right.

vocation director was very astute and asked him many well-crafted questions about his discernment. He could see clearly what puzzled his parents: Micah had never expressed an attraction to priesthood until very recently. What had changed? What happened? Micah was silent. Finally, under the inspiration of the Holy Spirit, the priest asked him, "Micah, have you committed some serious sin about which you are very sorry and ashamed?" The young man burst into tears and told him the whole story.

The priest worked with Micah and helped him to find a good spiritual director who could guide him to have peace and to accept the forgiveness of Christ. He told Micah that he was not ready to go to the seminary. He must go to the seminary only for the right reasons, and feeling badly about a particular sin is not a good reason to become a priest.

Micah told his parents that his "acceptance" had been deferred due to his poor grades. He was to go to college for a couple of years to prove he was capable of the academic requirements of seminary. While this was true enough, it was not the whole truth. Micah was pursuing priesthood for the wrong reason. Not knowing the whole truth, Micah's parents were very angry with the vocation director and they wrote him a letter to express their disappointment.

Scenario 4: Tim – A Son's Decision

Tim was an excellent student, especially in math and science. He was also handsome, polite, athletic, and popular. He had a well-grounded faith and said his prayers faithfully, attended Mass and showed sincere interest in his relationship with Jesus. His parents could not have been any more proud of him.

Tim's father was a structural engineer and owned a very successful engineering firm which specialized in building bridges. Tim excelled through high school academically and athletically, and his parents were thrilled when he began to talk about attending the best engineering school in the state. They had every expectation that he would do well and come back to join his father in the firm.

During college, away from home for the first time, Tim experienced a radical conversion and he began to attend daily Mass and to seek holiness. He went on several retreats and sought out spiritual direction from the chaplain at the Catholic campus ministry. At Christmas during his sophomore year, Tim told his parents that he had decided to go to the seminary beginning that fall.

His parents were very upset about this. They argued that he should finish his engineering studies first because he was already half way completed. Then he could go on to seminary if he chose, and if he decided to leave seminary, he could come back to a lucrative position very easily. Tim promised that he would consider carefully what they had said. He agreed to take this back to spiritual direction and prayer, and he did so. But he was very uneasy about it. After much prayer and discernment, he still felt strongly that he was called to be a priest. He felt that to delay going to the seminary would be to say no to Christ. By the end of the semester, he had made his decision. His parents were very disappointed, but they loved him and they were still proud of him. They both promised to do their best to support him.

These four scenarios illustrate how every man's personal past and maturity level is different, and these factors are very important when answering the two questions: Should I go to seminary? When should I go?

"Consider if your teenage son had the ambition — and the ability — to become an architect. Most parents would encourage this interest, even going out of their way to research the best colleges for architecture. But the same parents — even good Catholic moms and dads — express reservations about their son attending seminary. Why would you encourage your son to learn how to build roads and bridges, but discourage him because he wants to build the Kingdom of God?"[11]

from Vocation Mythbusters for Parents

Undue Influence

"But how can I be sure that my son has not been unduly pressured or influenced to go to seminary?" I commiserate with parents who ask this question. Yes, as a parent, it *is* your duty and prerogative to ask questions and to make certain that your need less input from parents regarding life decisions. But if he is seventeen and a senior in high school, I encourage parents to ask a lot more questions and to help him make sure that he has covered all the bases. Parents can intuit when people and circumstances have influenced their son in an unhealthy manner, and it is the parent's duty to protect him. On the other hand, just because a young man has been inspired to consider priesthood by a happy priest, that does not mean that he has been *unduly* influenced.

What about a Marketable Degree?

What degree(s) will my son get in the college seminary and what degree in major seminary? And if he leaves seminary, will he be marketable? Will he be able to get a job?

A student in college seminary will usually earn an undergraduate degree in philosophy. Some college seminaries, depending on how they are set up, offer degrees in other areas, like economics, business, humanities, and computer science. The PPF (The Program for Priestly Formation; produced by the U.S. Conference of Catholic Bishops) requires that a man earn thirty-six credit hours in undergraduate philosophy and twelve credit hours in undergraduate theology prior to beginning major seminary. It is challenging to take major courses in another area and still obtain these theology prerequisites.

Is a philosophy degree marketable? Learning to think and reason clearly (philosophy) is a very appropriate preparation both for further studies and for life itself. Whether this man continues in seminary to become a priest or leaves to continue professional studies or enter the workforce, his formation and education is invaluable. A well-rounded education is useful in every field. I have known seminarians who left college seminary and successfully pursued advanced degrees in other fields. Learning to think and reason clearly, in the light of God's Revelation, is a very appropriate preparation for living a successful, balanced life!

In major seminary, a man will receive at a minimum the Master of Divinity degree. This is the ordination degree. Many men will also earn an STB (Bachelor of Sacred Theology) or an MA in Theology with a concentration in a specific area of study (Systematic Theology, Moral Theology, Scripture, etc.). These theological degrees are highly specialized in the Catholic theological tradition and would not be of much direct use in areas outside of the Church. However, if a man finishes this degree and chooses not to be ordained a priest, his degree qualifies him to teach at the high school or college level in a Catholic institution.

God is quite capable of giving your son professional or financial success, regardless of his college degree. Psalm 127 makes this point well: "In vain is your earlier rising, your going later to rest, you who toil for the bread you eat: when he pours gifts on his beloved while they slumber." Trust in the providence of God. He loves your son infinitely more than you do, and has a great plan for his overall "success" in life.

"To have beautiful and holy thoughts, to write books on the lives of the saints, all of this does not count so much as answering as soon as you are called."[12]

St. Therese of Lisieux

What if My Son Leaves Seminary?

"If my son leaves college seminary, will he be able to resume his college studies without losing too much time?"

College seminaries are accredited institutions, and thus their credits will usually transfer to most colleges and universities. If your son takes his core classes in a college seminary, most of these credits will transfer to the core classes in another college. Once he begins taking a lot of philosophy and Catholic theology courses, these classes would be more difficult to place in the curriculum of a secular college. Every college has its own policies in this regard and the college registrar will be the one to determine which slots a given course might be able to fill in that degree curriculum.

Some parents have said to me: "This is why I think my son should wait until he finishes college. He needs to have an ordinary college experience and get a degree which could actually get him a paying job. Then if he wants to be a priest, he can go. And his college degree will help him run the business

If your son is called to be a priest, he has been greatly honored by God. He has been chosen to do something extraordinary. If he realizes this call at a young age, he needs to respond to it. Timing is very important. I have worked with men whom I was convinced had vocations to priesthood, but they decided (with the strong encouragement of their parents) not to go to college seminary immediately. These men went to a secular college, had the "ordinary college experience," which is often *not* good Christian formation, and they lost their vocations. One married man told me, "Not going to seminary as soon as I heard the call cost me my vocation to priesthood, and I regret that. I love my wife and children, but I was called to be a priest."

"Angelo Roncalli kept a spiritual journal of his inner life for more than 60 years. At one point he wrote: 'I do not remember a time when I did not want to be a priest.' He entered the seminary in 1892 in nearby Bergamo at the age of 11. He was elected Pope on October 28, 1958 and chose the name Pope John XXIII. He became known as 'the Good Pope' and 'The Parish Priest of the World.'"[13]

Shouldn't He Date First?

Should a man date before he goes to seminary, so that, as some people say, "he will know what he is giving up?" Dating can help a person mature by working on good relationships, growing in selflessness, appreciating others' families, and improving one's manners. However, dating is not necessarily a requirement for those discerning priesthood. We all know that most dating today, because of the over-sexualization of our culture, is not pure. Young people often have sexual experiences very early, as this is programmed into them by the media and peer culture. Even if a young man very much intends to date purely, the woman he dates may not have that same understanding and formation. Does sexual activity make a man better prepared to be a priest? No. Sin is never a good preparation for anything. Certainly God can use men who have sexual experiences in their history and make them into excellent priests. And yes, they likely will be more merciful with others as a result of their own history of sin and mercy.

Nonetheless, this does not make sin a good preparation for priesthood. What happens more often, in my experience, is what happened to the married man I mentioned above. He falls in love with a woman, or he is so confused because of sexual activity that he thinks he is in love, and he moves towards marriage. And then the man later regrets that he did not answer the call to seminary when he received it. (Incidentally, sin is not a good preparation for Holy Marriage either.)

Going to seminary early will result in a better formed, more mature, more faith-filled, more generous adult Christian man, even if he has not dated. Going to secular college first will not accomplish this to the same degree. If a man goes to college seminary immediately, God will guide that man to leave seminary at the appropriate time, if he is not called to be a priest. God has a plan for your son and it will be effective!

Going to a Regular College First

I know many seminarians and priests who went to ordinary college first, like myself. And like myself, they survived, though not completely unscathed, and were ordained priests. These men certainly bring all of their education and experiences to priesthood, and their college degrees are part of this. Perhaps in some ways, they are better priests because of it, but this is not to say that all those who go to ordinary college first become better priests. That is simply not true. Some men are not ready to go to seminary early and they did the right thing by waiting. God asks different things of different men at different seasons of their lives. Parents, God is calling you to trust him with the life and vocation of your son.

Mom and dad, I know this may make you nervous. Please remember that seminary formation is the absolute best education and formation that the Catholic Church has to offer! Whether he continues on and ends up being ordained a Catholic priest or not, he will leave seminary a much better formed, virtuous, dependable, well-integrated man of God. Going to the seminary will do nothing but help your son. It will not hurt him!

"If we open ourselves totally to Jesus, are we not afraid that He might take something away from us? He takes nothing away, and he gives you everything."[14]

Pope Benedict XVI

I always advise parents to ask themselves this very sober question: "Am I doing my job as a parent by cautioning my son to be prudent and wait to go to seminary? Or am I advising him in this way because I really don't want him to be a priest, and I am hoping that he will meet a girl, get a job and change his mind?" Some honest parents might reply: "That's a good question. I better go pray about that before I answer it."

The Father of Msgr. Marvin LeFrois

The oldest priest in the Diocese of Savannah is Msgr. Marvin LeFrois. He grew up on an apple orchard near Rochester, New York. His father had a thriving business harvesting and drying apples for widespread distribution. As teenagers and young men, Marvin and his three brothers were an integral part of the labor-intensive business.

In the 1930s, the oldest brother, Vincent, felt a call to the priesthood. He attended seminary not far from the orchard, and would help out in the summers. "But I remember when Vince was ordained a priest, he stopped helping us in the dry house, which was the special building where my dad dried the apples," related Msgr. LeFrois.

Remarkably, the next oldest brother, Joseph, also felt called to priesthood. He joined the Josephite Order, moving to the rural South to serve African-American communities. He was much too far away to help with the family business.

The next brother, Chris, also became a priest. He joined the Benedictines. He served as a chaplain in the Air Force in the years following World War II. Helping in the dry house was out of the question.

Eventually Marvin, too, entered the seminary and he became a priest in what was then a far-flung mission, the Diocese of Savannah. Like his other brothers, upon ordination he stopped helping in the dry house.

"I was the last to be ordained," said Msgr. LeFrois, "After my ordination, a reporter asked my dad what he thought of all his sons becoming priests. He answered, 'Well, my sons have all gone to God, but my business has gone to hell!"

CHAPTER 7

APPLYING TO SEMINARY

"Six months! You've got to be kidding me!"

"No," I replied, "I'm not." I was in my office with a young man who had just finished his official interview with me. It had gone well. He was a good candidate for seminary. As the vocation director, I then invited him to complete the formal application process. He was shocked at how long it would take.

I have known seminarians who were high-ranking military officers, CEOs of large corporations, and members of the Secret Service. Most said the application process to become a priest was at least as rigorous as in their previous high-level positions.

This was not always so. In days gone by, the local pastor would bring in a young man to see the seminary rector, saying, "This young man wants to be a priest. I know him and his family well. He's a good boy. I'm leaving him with you." That was about it! The pastor's recommendation was all that was required.

In our current, highly mobile society, a much more thorough screening process is essential. The pastor's recommendation is still important, but it is only one part of the application. I think we all know how important the proper screening of our future priests is to the well-being of the Church.

In order to become a diocesan priest, a man cannot simply download an application from the diocesan website, fill it out, and send it in. The vocation director must know this man *well* before he ever begins the application process, usually because the man has attended vocation retreats and other discernment events. The initial application form is quite extensive, but it is only the beginning of the application process.

1. **Multi-page application form.** The first requirement in the process is to fill out a lengthy application form, much like an application for employment, except more extensive.

2. **Physical exam.** A physical exam is required from a local physician. The Church wants assurance that this man has the physical health to function as a diocesan priest and

that, all things being equal, he will live to serve as a priest for many years.

3. **Psychological exam.** The actual psychological exam may last anywhere from one full day to a week. The vocation director usually sets this up with a pre-approved psychologist who knows which tests to conduct and exactly what kind of an assessment is desired. The purpose, generally speaking, is to have assurance that the man is psychologically and emotionally stable enough to function as a priest. The exam rules out psychosis and looks very carefully at a man's psycho-sexual development. The final written report is sent to the vocation director, though the candidate may receive an oral review of the findings in a follow-up appointment with the examiner. This process can last several months because it is often difficult to get an appointment for these lengthy evaluations. The final written report can take several weeks or more to arrive.

4. **Transcripts.** The candidate must send for official transcripts of all academic work beginning in high school and including all college and post-graduate work.

5. **Sacramental records.** Newly issued certificates of all sacramental records are to be sent directly from the church where the sacrament was received to the vocation office. This includes Baptism, first Holy Communion, and Confirmation.

6. **Autobiography.** Usually the candidate is required to write an autobiography covering his entire life up to the present. Each diocese will give specific instructions in regard to length, areas to be covered, etc. These documents are usually quite lengthy.

7. **Letters of recommendation.** Reference letters usually are sought from people who have known the candidate in a variety of life situations, at different times in his life. These would include a parent or family member, a co-worker, a teacher, a coach, a friend, his pastor, another priest he knows well, etc.

8. **Vocation Committee interview.** Some dioceses require that each candidate interview with a diocesan vocation committee, a group composed of the vocation director, other priests, religious and lay people.

9. **Background check.** Most dioceses today will require a criminal background check and credit check of the candidate.

Because it is so extensive, this application process can last many months, depending on how motivated the candidate is and how quickly he can get assessment appointments. It is usually assumed (or at least hoped) by both the vocation director and the candidate that he is likely to be accepted, which is why he was invited to apply in the first place. However, my strong advice for parents and family members is to keep this application process "in the family" until it is over. Try not to talk about it too much! Don't tell the neighbors or parishioners. Sometimes something is discovered during the application process which precludes the man from being accepted, or at least it delays acceptance. If this happens, it can be embarrassing to the man, all the more if it has been talked up all over town. There is no hurry to tell the world that your son wants to be a priest. Let him get accepted by the diocese first!

I heard of a certain pastor who was thrilled that a young man from his parish was finally going to the seminary. The pastor talked about it constantly. He put his name in the bulletin, prayed for him in the Prayers of the Faithful, and even put a message of congratulations on the billboard in front of the church! The man was not accepted. It was terribly awkward for the man, for his family, and for the pastor.

What kinds of things could trigger non-acceptance or delay?

If a man's transcripts indicate weak academic work, the vocation director may want him to complete another year of college to improve his grades and prepare for master's level studies. Sometimes there is an issue raised by the psychological exam which needs therapeutic attention prior to beginning depression, an illness which he has never addressed, and it inhibits him from doing his best work. The psychologist may recommend a more thorough evaluation and some counseling and treatment before he is placed in the seminary environment. Perhaps evidence comes out through the application process that the man is struggling more than he should with chastity, and he needs a longer period of sexual sobriety (continence) before he can begin priestly formation. This is why it is so important for the man to have a close relationship with the vocation director, and to tell him everything. If he does this, there will be no surprises during the application process.

If he is not initially accepted, does this mean that he can never become a priest?

It depends on the issue and the progress that the man is able to make. If the vocation director suspects a man has a genuine call, he will help him deal with his issues so that he can succeed in the seminary and be ordained a priest. I have seen seminarians who were not initially accepted, but who dealt with their formation issues, then later entered the seminary and did very well.

Of course, some issues are just fatal. If a man has a sexual attraction for minors, for example, he will never be accepted to go to seminary or to become a priest. If a man has a serious psychosis of any kind, he cannot be accepted. The Church needs healthy priests!

Will my son feel like he has failed if he does not or cannot become a priest?

When an excited young man applies to a diocese and is not accepted, it is a great disappointment. Even if the acceptance is only deferred for a year or so, while he works on a certain issue, the young man will likely take it hard. During this time, it is important for the parents to encourage their son, to support him, and to assure him that God has a great plan for his life. When my spiritual directees endure disappointments regarding their vocations, I remind them of the words attributed to St. Vincent de Paul: "When going to the bishop or one's superior for a decision, remember that a yes is as good as a no." If a person really desires the will of God regarding their vocations, they trust that the Holy

Spirit will speak through the Church. Perhaps God does not want this man to go to the seminary to be a priest. Perhaps God does not want him to go quite yet. Maybe God wants this man to have some different experiences prior to beginning seminary, experiences which will help him become an even greater priest. Nothing happens without God's knowledge and permission. As Dante wrote, "In His will is our peace."

Once the entire application process is complete and the packet has all the required information, the dossier usually finds its way to the bishop's desk. Often, but not always, the process ends with an interview by the bishop of the diocese. Some bishops delegate the final authority to accept (or not to accept) to their vicar generals, vocation directors, or to vocation committees. If the diocese has its own seminary, the seminary rector and faculty will have a large say in acceptance.

Once the candidate is formally accepted, he will be assigned a seminary to attend. Every diocese gives seminary assignments in their own way, but the bishop usually makes the final call. Some dioceses do give candidates the opportunity to express their seminary preference and some do not. This is the beginning of the promise of obedience. The seminarian — for now "seminarian" is his official title — goes where he is sent. This is how the Catholic Church works. It started with the apostles. Priests go where they are sent. This is emphasized every day in the Holy Mass. The words, in Latin, with which every Mass ends are "*Ite missa est.*" These words mean, "Go, you are sent forth!" The word *missa* is likewise the etymological root for our English word missile. A priest is sent forth, and when he lands, he is to set the world on fire for Jesus!

It should be noted that once the seminary assignment is received, the seminarian must complete yet another application, the one for the specific seminary. However, most of the required information which must accompany this application has already been gathered through the diocesan application process. ·

Your son is now finally going to the seminary! Going to the seminary does not mean that he will definitely end up becoming a priest. However, in the seminary, he will be able to definitively discern his correct vocation. The only place a man can finally and confidently know whether or not he should become a priest is in

The Mother of Cardinal Francis Xavier Nguyen van Thuan

Cardinal Francis Xavier Nguyen van Thuan was a Vietnamese bishop who spent thirteen years in a Communist prison camp, with nine years in solitary confinement. He remained steadfastly faithful to Jesus Christ and the Catholic Church.

After his release, he was invited by Pope John Paul II to give the Lenten retreat to the papal household. The retreat was so inspiring, it was lauded throughout the world! The transcript of the retreat eventually became a famous book titled *Testimony of Hope*. After the cardinal's death, his cause for canonization was opened and it continues today.

This is what this saintly priest and bishop wrote in the preface of *Testimony of Hope*:

> To my mother Elizabeth
> Who educated me from the time I was in her womb.
> She taught me stories from the Bible every night;
> She told me the stories of our martyrs,
> Especially of our ancestors;
> She taught me love for my country;
> She presented St. Therese of the Child Jesus
> As the model of Christian virtue.
> She was the strong woman who buried her brothers,
> massacred by traitors whom she sincerely pardoned,
> always welcoming them as though nothing had happened.
> When I was in prison, she was my great comfort.
> She said to all, "Pray that my son will be faithful
> to the Church and remain where God wants him."[15]

CHAPTER 8

WHAT IS SEMINARY LIKE?

Msgr. Steven Rohlfs, the rector of Mount St. Mary's Seminary where I used to work, has an interesting way of gauging the day-to-day health of the seminary. He says:

> "Each morning before I enter my office, I always check on two things. First, I look into the chapel to see if there are men praying before the Blessed Sacrament. Second, I walk through the hallways listening for the sounds of laughter. If these two things are present — prayer and joy — I know all is well at the seminary."

I think that most people, including most Catholics, have an idea that a seminary is like a strict monastery. Perhaps they have seen a movie in which the monks are walking around in complete silence, fingering their rosary beads, chanting in Latin, and never smiling or laughing. That idea is not true even of a monastery, and it is certainly not true of a seminary. Seminaries in the U.S. are very much like specialized universities such as medical schools or law schools. They exist to train men to do specialized work which requires not only academic knowledge, but also the development of the skills to do their work: to bring Jesus to people and people to Jesus. The priesthood is not a job; it is a *life*. Seminarians must be formed not just to *do* something but to *be* someone — someone very extraordinary. Seminarians must be formed to be an *alter Christus* — another Christ.

It is true that a Catholic seminary is a place of deep prayer, and that necessitates a certain amount of silence, but it is also true that seminaries are places of great joy and excitement. Seminarians study hard, they pray hard, they serve other people, and they have fun. Laughter rings in the halls of our seminaries because the men are joyful. They are excited to be following Jesus and excited that they might be called to become priests. I consider it one of the greatest privileges of my life to have lived in a house with one hundred fifty men who were seriously trying to become like Jesus.

A Transformation of Seminaries

I have visited nearly every diocesan seminary in the country, and I always come away impressed. In my opinion, today's seminaries are very healthy and holy places for a man to live and grow.

This has not always been the case, even in my lifetime. In the 1970s and 1980s, there were some unhealthy seminaries in the U.S., places where the theology was deficient. They were places of de-formation as much as formation. More than one priest from this era told me that he became a priest not because of the seminary he attended, but in spite of it.

Since the 1990s, I have witnessed a magnificent transformation in the majority of diocesan seminaries. This was largely due to the intervention of Pope John Paul II, who instituted "Apostolic Visitations" of every seminary in the U.S. A team of specially-chosen bishops, priests, and lay theologians visited every seminary in the country and conducted an extensive evaluation. They examined the entire formation program and interviewed all faculty members and students. The seminaries which really needed improvement were told very clearly to clean up their acts.

I believe the second factor which triggered this transformation was the seminarians themselves. A new wave of young men wanted to become holy priests who were generous and completely orthodox in Catholic teaching. They wanted to be kind, good shepherds. And they practically demanded that they be trained in this way!

I studied at the same seminary where I later worked, and I was ordained a priest in the diocese of Savannah in 1991. At my ordination, I really believed that I had received marvelous formation. I felt well-prepared to serve God as a priest in today's culture. However, I would say that the formation in today's seminaries is *vastly superior* to what I received. I credit Pope John Paul II and his important document *Pastores Dabo Vobis* (I Will Give You Shepherds), upon which every priesthood formation program in the world is now based.

Let me repeat: the formation of future priests is the finest education the Catholic Church has to offer. Now is a great time to go to the seminary to become a priest!

---

*"The formation of future priests... is considered by the Church to be
one of the most demanding and important tasks for the future of the
evangelization of humanity."*[16]

Pope St. John Paul II

Eight to Ten Years of Formation

Before ordination a man must complete at least four years of
master's-level formation. This formation period is called Major
Seminary or Theology. Prior to this, he must have a college
degree and two years of Philosophy, which is completed either in
college seminary or, if a man already has a degree, in a special
two-year program called Pre-Theology.

This process may seem like it takes a long time, but it is
important that your son be well-formed. Parents sometimes say:
"In that amount of time, he could be a medical doctor with a
specialization, making a large salary! Is all of that education
necessary to become a priest?" Yes, it is. And your son *will* be a
doctor—a doctor of souls. This is why the Church traditionally
refers to a priest as a "curate." He will be a specialist in healing
people of sin and bringing them to Jesus Christ.

The Four Pillars of Formation

In *Pastores Dabo Vobis*, Pope John Paul II prescribed four
dimensions of priestly formation, sometimes called the "four
pillars": Spiritual, Human, Intellectual, and Pastoral. Let's look at
each briefly.

Spiritual Formation. Most seminarians pray between three
and four hours a day, which includes Mass, a personal holy hour,
the liturgy of the hours, the rosary, and other devotions. It also
includes regular retreats and seeing a spiritual director two to
four times per month. You may be thinking, "My son will never
be able to do that. He can't sit still for fifteen minutes." It is true
that grace builds on nature, but grace is very powerful. When I
worked in a seminary, I would see fifty new seminarians begin

Human Formation. Your son will be challenged to grow into a courteous, generous Christian gentleman. The basic principle of human formation is found in *Pastores Dabo Vobis* #43: "The human personality of the priest is to be a bridge and not an obstacle for others in their meeting with Jesus Christ the Redeemer of the human race." Some men arrive at seminary with better human formation than others, but all have work to do before being ordained. Human formation includes, for example, how a man dresses, how he interacts with others, and how he speaks. It includes personal hygiene, table manners, and the skillset to deal kindly with difficult people. Human formation includes how to shake hands like a man in the U.S. culture (firmly and strongly). It includes shaping his persona so that he will be attractive and approachable to others. Good human formation means that a candidate acts manly, but kindly. He smiles often and laughs. He knows how to make true friends and he knows how to set appropriate boundaries in his relationships. Human formation includes appropriate use of alcohol, tobacco, or other substances. It includes exercise, weight loss, and personal appearance. The seminarian is constantly reminded that "most people buy the product because they like the salesman." While a priest should not be understood as a salesman, he does need to be attractive and persuasive to bring Jesus and his teachings to the world.

What other graduate schools do you know that help a man to grow in human formation like this? This is extraordinarily valuable, whether or not he ends up becoming a priest.

Intellectual Formation. Your son will take a carefully planned succession of philosophical and theological courses during his six to eight years in seminary. He will take courses in philosophy, Sacred Scripture, Church History, Dogmatic (or Systematic) Theology, Psychology, Counseling, Classical Languages (Latin, Hebrew, Greek), necessary Pastoral Languages (Spanish), Moral Theology, Liturgy, Music—and practica to teach him how to celebrate Mass, hear confessions, and celebrate the other sacraments. He will learn all the teachings of the Catholic Church on faith and morals, where these teachings come from in Scripture and Tradition, and why they are true. Give him a few years, but he will be able to articulately explain the teachings of the Catholic Church by the time he is finished. Yes, that includes the difficult teachings.

Pastoral Formation. Your son will be sent out to practice his newly acquired skills. He will be sent on "apostolate" (his pastoral assignment) to visit a hospital, to teach Catechism in a school, to work in ministry with a certain ethnic group, to visit shut-ins, to visit prisoners, etc. The seminary will make sure that he has both training and experience in each of these ministries. During these apostolates, the seminarian will learn that he has a special interest and special gifts in some areas of priestly work and needs improvement in others.

In his final year of seminary, as a transitional deacon, he will be assigned to a parish where he will be given the opportunity to preach, to witness marriages, and to baptize. He is now getting very close to priestly ordination and he should be confident (in a humble, Christ-centered kind of way) that he can do the work of a priest.

A Full-time Endeavor

St. Vincent de Paul once wrote: "There is nothing more perfect than the formation of a good priest." Being formed as a priest is hard work. Thus a seminarian is in seminary full-time. The Church wants to be sure that this man understands exactly what priesthood entails, and that he will be confident that he can live priesthood in tranquility of mind and heart. This is why the formation program is so long and rigorous. Still, a seminarian has free time to relax and enjoy life. Weekends are free and the seminarians come and go as they desire when there are no seminary commitments.

Serious "Dating"

Going to the seminary is analogous to a young man who begins to seriously date a young woman, to the exclusion of all others. They like each other very much and have great hopes that they will marry. No one is setting a date, reserving the church, or buying a wedding dress just yet. We all know that sometimes these relationships don't work out, and that does not mean that anyone has done anything wrong. We certainly hope that things

We also know that in the great plan of God some men are called to go to the seminary who are not called to become priests. God orchestrates it all for the good of the Church.

Summer Assignments

During the summers, except for a few weeks of vacation, most seminarians receive an assignment from their vocation director to work in a parish, hospital, or some other pastoral assignment. These summer internships are an essential part of preparing this man for the pastoral work of a priest. Normally, the diocese gives a living stipend to help the seminarian during this training.

Installation of Ministries

In major seminary, a seminarian receives certain official ministries as benchmarks of his growing confidence that he is called to be a priest. These ministries are Lector, Acolyte, and Candidacy. Lector makes a man an official reader of the Sacred Scriptures at Mass. As an Acolyte, a man moves closer to the sacred mysteries and he begins to serve Holy Mass regularly. This ministry grants him a universal office as an extraordinary minister of the Eucharist. And Candidacy is a declaration from the seminarian that he is committing himself to diocesan priesthood in the diocese for which he is studying. These ministries may be given in one's home diocese by the local bishop or in the seminary, and the order in which they are received may vary. Family members are invited to these ceremonies and encouraged to come celebrate these important benchmarks.

Ordinations

In most seminaries, after a man's third year of Theology (five to seven years after beginning seminary), a man is ordained a transitional deacon (since he will be transitioning to priesthood soon). At this ordination, the man is making a final promise to embrace celibacy. He also makes permanent and binding promises to pray every day the Liturgy of the Hours (the prayer book of every priest consisting of psalms and other Scripture readings), and he makes a promise of respect and obedience to his bishop. This ordination may take place at the seminary or in his home diocese. Parents and family members should plan to attend this ordination, as it is the culmination of a lot of study, prayer, and work.

Note that a transitional deacon is distinguished from a permanent deacon in the Catholic Church. Every man moving towards priesthood must be first ordained a transitional deacon. However, some men, including married men, are called to be ordained permanent deacons in the Church.

Finally, after his fourth year of Theology (six to eight years after beginning seminary), a man is ordained a priest. This ordination Mass is almost always held at the cathedral of the man's home diocese and the ordination is celebrated by the local bishop. The next day, the newly ordained priest celebrates his first Mass, which is called his Mass of Thanksgiving. Both the priesthood ordination and the Mass of Thanksgiving should be attended by the parents and the entire family.

Note that the Sacrament of Holy Orders is the only sacrament in the Catholic Church which has three different levels: deacon, priest, and bishop. Your son will receive his first ordination when he is ordained a transitional deacon. Then after he has "practiced" that ministry for six to twelve months, he advances to the order of priesthood. This is his second ordination.

For most men, this will be the final ordination of his life. However, some few will be chosen by the Holy Father later in life to become bishops. These men will receive a third ordination, the third level of Holy Orders. Only a bishop possesses the fullness of this sacrament.

Three Levels of Holy Orders and the Duties of Each

	Deacon	Priest	Bishop
Proclaim Gospel at Mass	Yes	Yes	Yes
Preach	Yes	Yes	Yes
Baptize	Yes	Yes	Yes
Witness Marriages	Yes	Yes	Yes
Hear Confessions		Yes	Yes
Celebrate Mass		Yes	Yes
Anoint the Sick		Yes	Yes
Confirm		Sometimes	Yes
Ordain			Yes

Family Weekends

Like colleges, most seminaries have family weekends. I highly recommend that you attend this weekend to see the environment in which your son lives.

I once read an article by a very ardent Protestant who visited his Catholic brother in seminary. This man was deeply skeptical of Catholicism, celibacy, and priesthood. After two days at the seminary, he radically changed his opinion. He was surprised by the authenticity of the seminarians. He described the men as joyful, intelligent, and deeply committed to Jesus.

I think when you visit your son's seminary, you will be similarly impressed. You will meet very fine, ordinary young men and hear lots of laughter. You will realize that seminarians are not prisoners. They have the freedom to get in their cars and go to the store or the movies. At the same time, you'll notice that the men take holiness seriously. They pray a lot, study hard, and make heroic efforts to grow in charity.

The word seminary comes from the Latin word *seminarium*, which means "seed-bed," a place where things can begin to grow. A seminary is like an atomic greenhouse where plants grow at a high rate of speed. You are going to see amazingly positive changes in your son over the next few years!

In my experience, parents usually leave the family weekend with a new feeling of confidence that their son is safe, in a wonderful place, and growing in knowledge and holiness. Some parents literally would say to me: "Father, this place is great! I need this in my own spiritual life. Can I come to the seminary too?"

The Father of St. Vincent de Paul

St. Vincent de Paul was born of peasant parents in a little village near Dax, France. His father could see that he was both pious and intelligent, so he made many sacrifices to send him to school to become a priest. In that day, priests led very privileged lives. St. Vincent was sent to Paris to study for the priesthood and he had been there for a few years, very much enjoying everything about it.

One day, his father arrived unexpectedly. He had walked all the way from Dax (two hours by bus, even today). He had come to visit his son, and he was hungry and exhausted, his ordinary peasant clothing covered with the dust of travel. Another seminarian answered the door and could not believe that this dirty peasant was Vincent's father. Vincent had become enamored by education, prestige, and fine dress, so when he saw how dirty and poorly clad his father was, he said, "I do not know him." His poor father was devastated and walked away sadly.

Soon after Vincent was ordained, he entered a crisis of faith. His ambition was to be comfortably well-off, which he achieved with a high-ranking and lucrative priestly assignment. But one day, he was celebrating holy Mass, and when he lifted up the chalice, he heard a voice very clearly say, "I tell you, I do not know you." His crisis of faith no doubt stemmed from his treatment of his father, but mostly it was caused by *the way he was living his priesthood*. He had been studying to become an ecclesiastic, not a priest of Jesus Christ. He was empty and depressed. As he later acknowledged, nothing is worse than a priest who knows his theology but does not know Jesus.

During this crisis of faith, Fr. Vincent was captured at sea by pirates and sold as a slave in Africa where he remained for three years. He suffered greatly during that time, and when he returned to Paris, he was a different priest. He immediately traveled to Dax to ask his father's forgiveness for denying him. He began to live his entire life in service to the poor, no longer as an ecclesiastic. St. Vincent de Paul later did great work in the rehabilitation of seminaries, so that future priests would truly love and serve Jesus, not themselves.

Chapter 9

WHO IS PAYING FOR ALL OF THIS?

Throughout the history of the Church, especially in poorer countries, the family was responsible for the cost of the priestly formation of their son. There is an older priest in my diocese whose mother sold her wedding ring to buy his theology books. Still today in some countries, I speak with seminarians who have had to leave the seminary and get a job for a while, precisely because their money ran out and their families were not able to help.

In the U.S. today, however, the bishop usually pays a seminarian's expenses, at least at the theology level. Of course, this money comes from the stewardship of the faithful people in that diocese. If a seminarian is in college seminary, the financial policy is usually different. Every diocese makes its own policy in this regard, and it is important to clearly understand your own diocesan policy before making any financial decisions. In this chapter, I will endeavor to answer some of the most commonly asked questions from parents of seminarians regarding finances.

If my son leaves the seminary, will he have to pay back the money the diocese spent on his education?

If your son leaves the seminary, after three years of study for instance, the diocese will have spent a large sum of money on his education. On average, a single seminarian costs more than $35,000 per year, which covers room, board, tuition, health insurance, stipend, etc. How would this man who had been in seminary three years ever pay back over $100,000? Most dioceses, in my experience, do not require this repayment, even though there may be an official repayment policy on the books somewhere.

When the bishop accepts a man to study to become a priest, the bishop is *investing* in that man, because he believes that he is called to be a leader in the Catholic Church. Remember that going to the seminary is the only place where a man can know definitively that he is being called to be a priest. He has been screened very carefully. The application process is thorough. The bishop is convinced of his goodness and faithfulness. If the man he will use his knowledge and formation to serve the Church as a devout layman. I know many former seminarians who are terrific lay leaders and evangelists. The bishop realizes this, and he understands that some men will be called by God to step out of seminary. For this reason, most dioceses do not ask a man who has left the seminary to repay the diocese what they have spent on his education and formation.

There is an even more important reason not to require repayment. If your son has been in seminary for a couple of years, and he has discerned carefully with his spiritual director that he should leave, he needs to leave! We don't want a man to stay in the seminary only because he fears he can never pay back the money he owes. This is a terrible conflict of interests, both for the Church and for the man. A man should never advance to ordination when he knows, deep inside, that he should not become a priest.

Sometimes when an older man, perhaps a widower who has been in business many years, makes the decision to become a priest, this man will offer to pay his own expenses. He reasons that since he has the financial resources, he might as well use them for his education and save the diocese some money. Many bishops will not permit this because "paying one's own way" might carry the misunderstanding of "having one's own way." The man needs to begin practicing obedience immediately, whether or not he has money. That being said, if a man leaves the seminary and then goes on to be very successful in business, there is nothing to stop him from making a generous contribution to the bishop's annual appeal.

Does the diocese support the seminarians monetarily while they are in seminary, or do the families have to support them?

Most dioceses support their graduate level seminarians by paying their tuition, room, board and health insurance, as well as a monthly living stipend. This stipend is usually quite modest, and seminarians are very grateful when their families can help them financially. But when their families cannot help them, the seminarian can still survive. The Knights of Columbus are extremely generous to seminarians with their RSVP program (Refund Support Vocations Program), granting nearly every seminarian in the U.S. a $500 annual stipend. Of course, it is not realistic for a seminarian to drive a new, expensive car with a high monthly payment and to go out to dinner three nights per week on his living stipend. The seminarian will need to simplify his life and live according to his means. This is sometimes difficult, especially if the man has been accustomed to a higher standard of living.

What does a man do if he has student loans to pay?

Depending on the type of loan, many student loans can be deferred until the man is ordained a priest and making a salary. Once ordained, the man will be able to make a modest monthly payment on his loans. It is true that some families have the means to repay student loans for their sons and some do not. If the man owes a very high amount of money in student loans, his bishop and vocation director may ask him to get a job and work for a couple of years, in order to pay down these loans, before they will allow him to begin seminary. It is very important that the Church always model the virtue of justice, which includes paying what we owe. The bishop will not want to give the impression that a man is running from his debts and the Church is helping him to do it.

If he needs money, can a seminarian hold a job while in the seminary?

The answer is almost always no. Priestly formation is full time work! Most seminarians need every hour of the day just to keep up with the demanding schedule of prayer, study, pastoral formation, and human formation. I suppose it is possible that a college seminarian might find the time to get a job working a few hours a week in the library or bookstore, but many rectors do not permit it. Once the man begins the last four years before ordination, it is very uncommon to have a job, even a small one. Priestly formation is too important and a man is expected to put all of his time and energy into this process.

Some seminarians have more monthly expenses than others. Some have physical illnesses or other medical conditions and they must purchase medicine, which can be very expensive even with good health insurance. I have known seminarians like this, and even though they lived very simply, they had to take out a expenses. A seminarian will always discuss this with his vocation director first and receive permission. After he is ordained a priest, he begins to make monthly payments on these loans.

If a seminarian has student loans or other loans that cannot be deferred while he is in seminary, he must be able to make the monthly payments on these loans. If he cannot, he cannot begin seminary. Every seminarian should be completely transparent with his vocation director during the application process regarding any and all debts. The vocation director will know the policy of the diocese in this regard.

Where will the seminarian be assigned during the summers? Is he permitted to get a summer job and make money?

Some vocation directors permit college-level seminarians to go home and get a job during the summer. But more and more often, in my experience, seminarians are given pastoral assignments which are part of their priestly formation. Seminarians are given a variety of summer assignments, varying from working in a parish, ministering in a hospital, or studying Spanish in another country. Seminarians usually receive their summer assignment from the vocation director or the seminary faculty, with the knowledge and permission of the bishop.

Do seminarians get a vacation? Once ordained, do priests get a vacation and time off on a regular basis? Who pays for this vacation?

Every seminarian is given vacation time in the summer, usually a couple of weeks. Once ordained, every priest is permitted by Canon Law to take up to four weeks of vacation per year. Some priests choose to take this vacation time all at once and others take a week here and there. The priest is free to spend this vacation as he chooses. Some take time with their families, many travel with other priests, and some just go to a private place for relaxation, reading, and prayer.

Priests must pay for their own vacations in full, though they are still receiving their salary during those four weeks. Some priests save their money so that they can travel widely during their vacation time and others like to stay closer to home. Cruise lines are regularly looking for priests to celebrate daily Mass on their ships, and some priests take these free cruises for vacation!

In addition to this vacation time, every priest is strongly encouraged to take off one day each week. Depending on distance, the priest can go spend time with his family and friends, or he can just relax, hike, play golf, or run errands.

After Mass on the major feast days, like at Christmas and Easter, many priests take a few days off to rest and recuperate. This is yet another opportunity when seminarians and priests can spend quality time with their families.

How do diocesan priests get paid? Will he need financial support from his family?

Diocesan priests in the U.S. receive a modest monthly salary, usually paid by their parish assignment. Normally between $1,500-$2,000 per month, this amount can differ slightly from diocese to diocese, and some dioceses give a small increase to priests who have been ordained a certain number of years, serve as pastors, etc.

In addition, as part of their salary packages, diocesan priests ordinarily receive health insurance, automobile expenses, and room and board in the parish rectory. All of this is paid for by the parish or institution where he is assigned. The philosophy behind this system is that priests do not have to worry about money, so that they can give themselves completely to serving God and others. If they are living simply as a priest should, they generally have more than enough for their personal needs and wants.

Priests also receive gifts from the people in their parishes, along with stipends for Masses, weddings, baptisms, and funerals. The priest is usually able to use this money as he chooses, though some dioceses require that these stipends be turned over to the parish. It is true that some priests have exceptional circumstances which require more money, such as a priest who has a medical condition which requires doctors' visits, hospitalizations, and medicine. The bishop will work with any priest who has these types of liabilities and help him to survive financially.

Do priests receive good health insurance?

Both seminarians and priests are placed on the diocesan health care policy. Usually, a seminarian's premium is paid by the diocese, while a priest's premium is paid by the parish where he is assigned. People are very kind and generous to their priests especially if they get sick, and they are well-cared for medically by the doctors and nurses in their parishes, often at little or no cost!

Do priests receive a retirement plan as part of their compensation?

Every U.S. diocese has a retirement package for its priests. The parish of assignment pays into this plan monthly and it is well-protected. Many priests these days also have their own IRA or some tax-free retirement plan, but they must pay into this plan with their own money. Because the IRS considers priests as self-employed, their self-employment tax goes toward Social Security, which they can draw at the appropriate age.

At what age can a priest retire?

A priest is usually required to retire at the age of seventy-five, and many may retire at sixty-five or seventy. Each bishop has his own policy in this regard, and it often depends on the number of priests who are available to staff his parishes. If a priest asks to retire at sixty-five or seventy, this request will at least be considered by the bishop. If the priest is healthy, the bishop may refuse to accept his retirement, and strongly encourage the priest to work a few more years because the need is so great. According to Canon Law, a bishop cannot refuse the request of a priest to retire when the priest is seventy-five. Many U.S. priests semi-retire, working in parishes as associate priests but no longer responsible for the administration of parishes. I do know some priests who have willingly continued to work as a pastor after the age of seventy-five, with their bishops' consent. Usually, the bishop is thrilled that a priest is willing to keep helping him staff his parishes, even in his advanced age. Obviously, when a priest gets too sick or feeble to do parish work, he must retire.

Where do priests live when they retire?

Some dioceses have built very nice retirement centers for their priests. Others simply let the retired priests live where they choose. Priests can be very independent fellows. They often want to live in the same city where they spent most of their lives working as a priest, because it is where their friends and loved ones live. These priests do not want to leave their hometown to go live in a priest retirement center in another city where they do not know anyone. Some really enjoy living with other retired priests, and some prefer to live alone. A retired priest is free to live anywhere that he can afford, and some become "snow-birds" moving to warm-weather states. However, his brother diocesan priests are very grateful when a priest decides to retire nearby. Retired priests are a great blessing to active priests: for spiritual direction, for confession, for their experience and priestly wisdom, and for covering Masses and funerals during vacation.

Bishops will always take care of their priests when they get old and sick, even if the priest's personal retirement funds run out. They will be provided for and cared for medically and otherwise, and they will receive a dignified Catholic burial when they die. Priests take care of the Church and the Church takes care of priests.

Can a priest receive financial gifts/inheritances or would that money all go to the diocese?

A diocesan priest does not make a vow of poverty. Therefore, he is free to accept financial gifts and to inherit property or resources from his family. This is his money and he can dispose of it as he chooses. It is theoretically possible for a priest to be a millionaire, because of family inheritance, and he is under no obligation to give this money to the diocese. On the other hand, a religious priest, a Franciscan for example, would not be free to inherit money or property, because of his vow of poverty. This inheritance would go directly to the Franciscan Order and be disposed of as the Superior directs. Some religious communities do permit the brother or sister to decide how the inherited money from their family will be given to the poor.

A diocesan priest is expected to work full time for the Kingdom of God. He typically would not be involved in a private business venture nor would he be able to run a family business on the side.

My son can barely balance his checkbook. Does the seminary teach a man how to financially administer a parish?

This is an excellent question, and bishops have been asking this same question of the seminaries to which they send their men. Today in many dioceses, a newly ordained priest can expect to become a pastor very quickly. Running a parish today is like being the CEO of a mid-size corporation, with a budget of a million dollars or more, many employees, and a large physical plant.

More and more seminaries are trying to incorporate classes or workshops for their men which will help them to step into their administrative role more peacefully. Due to education and prior work experience, some priests are better prepared for administration than others.

Besides these classes or workshops in the seminary, most dioceses provide workshops for their new priests, especially those who are becoming pastors. Every bishop has a diocesan business office, finance office, construction office, personnel office, etc., precisely to assist pastors in running the business side of parishes. These experts provide specific guidelines and personal oversight for parish finance reports, paying of chancery taxes, construction projects, contracts, hiring and firing, etc. They review every parish budget and conduct regular parish audits to ensure compliance. They guide the pastor in completing the necessary due diligence before hiring a new employee and the due process work before terminating an employee. The construction office oversees every step of design and construction of parish projects. Major contracts must be approved and signed by the bishop himself.

Finally, every individual parish has its own experts in finance, construction, architecture, and engineering. Priests are taught to rely heavily on these experts for guidance and advice as they make decisions regarding the business of the parish. These professionals in the parish love their parish and will do anything to help their priest make good decisions and to be a good steward of the parish finances — if they are asked!

Even if a young pastor has no formal education in business, finance, or administration, if he is wise and humble, he will ask the professionals in his parish and diocese for guidance. Through this guidance, he will learn to be a capable administrator of the parish, even if he can barely balance his checkbook!

Priests Honor Their Mothers and Fathers

Before the liturgical revisions after the Second Vatican Council, the *manuturgium* was part of the rite of ordination. The Latin word refers to a linen strip which was used to tie the newly-ordained priest's hands together after the anointing with sacred chrism. The linen was soaked with the sweet smell of the chrism, a smell that endured. A beautiful tradition developed that this *manuturgium* was kept as an important memento and given to the mother of the priest at the end of his first Mass. Then, when the mother died, the tradition was that her hands would be tied together as if in prayer with the chrism-soaked *manuturgium* in her casket—a powerful remembrance that she had given one of her sons to be a priest!

Though the *manuturgium* is no longer used in the actual ordination rite, many priests like to maintain a form of the tradition during the ordination by simply wiping the chrism from their hands on a specially-sewn linen cloth, sometimes inscribed with the name of the priest and the date of ordination. Though the cloth is not used to bind the priest's hands, it is still given to the mother at the first Mass, with the understanding that it will be placed in her casket with her when she dies, with the sweet smell of the sacred chrism still fragrant. This is not part of the ordination rite and it is certainly not required, though some priests choose to do it. It is a very beautiful and moving tradition for the mother of a newly ordained priest.

Similarly, a tradition has developed more recently in regard to the newly ordained priest's father. A priest may have a small, purple confessional stole monogrammed with his name and date of ordination. After hearing his first confession wearing this stole, he gives it to his father, often at the same first Mass.

Jared Seff

CHAPTER 10

OTHER FREQUENTLY ASKED QUESTIONS

There are many other vocation-related questions that parents and family members have asked me through the years. Here are a few of the most common.

Can my son come home from the seminary during Christmas, Easter, and Thanksgiving holidays? How much time should I expect him to spend with our family during these breaks?

As a seminarian, your son will usually be able to come home during these holiday times. As a priest, it is a bit harder, but most priests are able to get home right after the major celebrations are over and celebrate these great Christian feast days with their families. Once again, it depends on the distance they have to travel and the amount of time they have free. In my own experience as a priest, I am able to spend more time with my family at holiday times than my married siblings, since they have to split the vacation times with their in-laws.

Most seminaries I know are very generous with breaks during the Thanksgiving, Christmas and summer seasons. The seminarian is free to go home to his family during all of these breaks, as long as he can afford the travel arrangements and there is enough time to travel. Some seminaries do offer optional mission trips and other retreat or pilgrimage opportunities during breaks, and seminarians will try to take advantage of at least some of these. Many dioceses expect their seminarians to come home during Holy Week and Easter, specifically so as to serve the solemn Masses and other Holy Week liturgies. Also, breaks are a good time for seminarians to catch up on school work, to write papers, or to complete major projects. There will be many opportunities for your son to come home from the seminary each year, but he will have to make the prudential judgment on how to use these breaks.

What is the difference between a diocesan priest and a religious priest? What are the vows which all *religious* brothers and priests make?

A diocesan priest works in parishes and takes care of people hearing confessions, burying the dead. A diocesan priest promises to remain celibate, to pray for God's people, and to respect and obey his bishop (and his successors). A diocesan priest does not make a vow of poverty, so he can own things in his name, have a bank account, his own car, etc.

Religious priests, on the other hand, do not make the same three promises. They make the three *vows* of poverty, chastity and obedience, together called the Evangelical Counsels. These priests belong to particular religious orders, for example, the Franciscans, Jesuits, Dominicans, Salesians, Trappists, Benedictines, etc.

Jesus, the Son of God, lived perfectly these three Counsels and religious priests aspire to imitate Jesus in this regard. Therefore, the vow of poverty means that they cannot have their own bank accounts, own their own cars, computers, etc. That vow of poverty is very truly lived, but how it is lived can vary from among religious orders. Even their salaries from their pastoral work goes straight to the religious order and they are given living stipends for their necessities. Since they live together in a house with their other religious brothers, they eat together, recreate together, work together, etc. Thus they do not want and have no need for money in their pockets.

To use a medical analogy, diocesan priests are the general practitioners and religious priests are the specialists. Religious priests usually have a very specific apostolate (work) and a charism (spirituality) upon which their order was founded. The Dominicans were founded to preach. The Salesians were founded to help poor children. The Camillians were founded to nurse the sick. A man who joins a religious order typically finds himself very passionate about that specific, focused apostolate. A diocesan priest does a little bit of everything. He preaches, teaches, cares for the poor and the sick, buries the dead, and functions as the true father of the parish family. He is the family practitioner.

Also, religious priests almost always live together in a community and this community becomes their "new family." A diocesan priest, on the other hand, usually lives alone or with one or two other priests with whom he serves in a parish. A diocesan priest is not under a rule requiring him to work and pray with others, as he is sometimes the only priest around!

If my son is still unsure about priesthood while he is in the seminary, what will happen? What if he makes a sincere mistake when he discerns that he is being called to priesthood?

A man goes to the seminary one year at a time. He is not certain that he will be ordained a priest. At the end of every year, with the guidance of his spiritual director, rector, and vocation director, your son will decide if he should come back. Of course, the further along he continues, the higher the expectation is that he will follow through to priesthood. Most rectors and vocation directors would not encourage a man to come back for the third year of theology if he is still very much undecided about priesthood. A man is usually scheduled to be ordained a deacon at the end of third theology, so he should be convinced by that time! But remember, this man will have already been in seminary for at least four years before beginning third theology. That is a long time to study, pray, and weigh this decision carefully.

In chapter 2, I discussed the dual discernment that must take place *before* a man enters seminary. The man himself must discern that he is being called to take this step, and the Church, through the local vocation director and the bishop, must discern the same. In the seminary, this dual discernment continues. The man must still believe that he is called to be a priest, but the Church, through the formation faculty and the rector, must agree. Ultimately, only the bishop can call a man to Holy Orders, but the bishop entrusts the discernment and formation of his seminarians to the seminary formation team. This system functions as checks and balances, to be very sure that the man is really called to become a priest. The seminary faculty watches this man closely for six to eight years and they thoroughly evaluate him annually. This explains why some seminarians are asked to leave the seminary, even though they themselves may have wanted to stay. A man must experience the call to priesthood from God, and the Church must witness that call! All of this greatly reduces the possibility that a man will make a sincere mistake in his discernment.

Who exactly are the vocation director, the rector, and the spiritual director ? What are their jobs?

The vocation director is the local diocesan priest who represents the bishop in the diocese in the area of vocations. He is discerning priesthood. He organizes retreats and other vocation programs, and generally offers men good information about the priesthood. He is also usually the priest who guides the man through the application process and monitors his progress in the seminary.

Some dioceses have two priests assigned as vocation directors. One is the primary recruiter (though not in the sense of "talking men into" the seminary) and the other oversees the men once they are in the seminary. The latter visits them, gives them their summer assignments, encourages them, and challenges them in the areas in which they need to grow. Some vocation directors are full time and others are part time. In larger dioceses that have their own seminaries, the seminary rector assumes the responsibility for the man's formation.

In the Catholic Church, a *rector* is a person who holds the office of presiding over an ecclesiastical institution, (in this case, a seminary), for the local bishop. According to canon law, only the rector has the authority to accept a man to come to the seminary, to recommend promotion from year to year, and to recommend to the bishop that the man be ordained a priest. He is the only one who has the authority to expel. The rector has great authority in determining which men are approved to be priests. He operates in the *external forum*. This means that he must speak with the vocation director and bishop about the progress the man is making, or lack thereof. Of course, the bishop has complete freedom in deciding whom he will ordain a priest, but a wise bishop knows it is best to very seriously weigh the input of the rector before making this decision. The rector has watched each man day to day, for six years. He knows each man well, including his strengths and his weaknesses.

The spiritual director is a priest in the seminary who meets regularly with the candidate and talks about his spiritual life, prayer, overcoming sin, growing in virtue, etc. The spiritual director is a very important person in a seminarian's life. He listens carefully to the man's soul, hears his confessions, and helps him discern if Jesus really wants him to be a priest. The spiritual director operates completely in the *internal forum*. This is very similar to the seal of confession. The spiritual director never tells anyone — even the rector and the bishop — what he and the seminarian discuss. It is absolutely confidential between the two of them and the Lord.

You will hear your son speak often about these three priests — the vocation director, the rector, and the spiritual director — who are so influential in his priestly formation.

What will happen if my son decides to leave the seminary and not become a priest after a few years? Will there be a stigma attached to that?

In days gone by, there was a social stigma attached to a former seminarian. People might whisper, "That is the young man who went to the seminary to become a priest, but he came home. How embarrassing for his family. I wonder why they rejected him?" Today, there is a much more healthy and balanced view of discernment. Catholics understand in general that not every man who goes to the seminary becomes a priest, and that is fine. Some men are called by God out of the seminary after a few years, just as they were called by God into the seminary. Leaving the seminary does not necessarily mean that a man has done something wrong or that he has been rejected. He may have done everything right and been a model seminarian. It may mean that he has carefully discerned that God does not want him to become a priest. This decision usually comes from the advice of the seminary faculty and the man's own soul.

I have known seminarians who were excellent in every way, and as far I could see, would have been great priests. Some men simply did not have peace, even if they were doing everything right. They were praying faithfully, studying hard, and being completely honest with their spiritual directors. Their lack of peace continued for so long that eventually the seminary faculty agreed that they probably were not called to become priests. When a man would come to me as vice rector to give me the news that he was leaving formation, I would say, "Congratulations. I am proud of you. You obeyed God when he told you to come here. Now you are obeying him when he tells you to leave. Go, and become the saint you are called to be in your true vocation."

There is no longer a stigma when a man comes home from the seminary; most Catholics are very understanding in this regard.

How do we respond to people who express disapproval of our son's choice to go to the seminary? Or respond to people who assume that *we* are all saints because he is at seminary?

Having good information is important. With good information, you as parents will be able to articulately answer the questions and objections that others may have, especially since they are usually the same objections that you had. As you know so well, sometimes people ask questions or put their noses into other people's business when they should not. However, in my experience, when people ask questions or have concerns, it is usually because they sincerely care about the man and they want him to be happy and fulfilled. As a parent, you want that too!

When people ask you questions, you can quote the statistics that show that the huge majority of priests are happy and fulfilled. The huge majority of priests are selfless, holy, generous men who love Jesus Christ and his Church. And they spend themselves to love and take care of others in the name of Jesus. You can tell them that not every man who goes to the seminary becomes a priest. You can tell these sincere people who express disapproval, that you and your family are proud of your son. Let them know this in no uncertain terms!

With regard to people thinking that your family is the holiest family in town since you produced a seminarian, just smile and tell them the truth. God can call a man to be a priest out of any family, from the best to the worst. Of course you can say: "We are honored that God may be calling our son to be a priest."

How carefully does the diocese investigate the seminaries to which we send our men for their priestly formation? Who checks to be sure that the men are receiving orthodox, Catholic theology and sound spiritual direction?

Ultimately, the diocesan bishop must make the decision regarding which seminary or seminaries to use for the priestly formation of his men. If the diocese has its own seminary, then this is almost always where the men will study. However, the majority of U.S. dioceses do not have their own seminaries, so they must evaluate which seminaries to use. The vocation director is usually the one charged with visiting different seminaries and evaluating the formation programs in each. He brings this information to the bishop with his recommendations.

It should be noted that, just as different colleges and universities have different strengths and weaknesses, so do seminaries. Some seminaries are renowned for their solid, spiritual formation but not so well-revered for their academic work. Others are known for their excellent pastoral formation, but they seem to be weaker in the spiritual realm. Every bishop will think of the priestly strengths most needed in his respective diocese and he will send his men to the seminary which he thinks will most effectively produce that kind of priest. Some bishops have special pastoral needs in their dioceses, such as large populations of Spanish-speaking Catholics. This bishop may send his men to a seminary which has a strong reputation for teaching Spanish and training men how to minister to Hispanic people.

As I said above, most U.S. seminaries which train diocesan priests today have very solid formation programs. Parents can be sure that their sons are receiving an excellent theological and spiritual education, and that they will be well-prepared to function as balanced and orthodox Catholic priests.

What would happen if while in seminary my son meets a woman he would like to date?

Seminarians, like other men, are attracted to women; this is a normal part of being human. For six years I worked in a seminary which is located on a co-ed university campus. Often enough, seminarians would strike up friendships with college-aged women, with whom they shared the same dining hall. Some seminarians jokingly referred to these young women as "chalice chippers," because as you can imagine, occasionally a normal friendship would turn into something more. Sometimes a seminarian might even feel like he was falling in love. Is this a sign that he is not called to be a priest? Not necessarily. Here is what Cardinal Jorge Bergoglio, now Pope Francis, had to say about his experience when he was a young seminarian:

> "I was dazzled by a girl I met at an uncle's wedding... I was surprised by her beauty, her intellectual brilliance... and, well, I was bowled over for quite a while. I kept thinking and thinking about her. When I returned to the seminary after the wedding, I could not pray for over a week because when I tried to do so, the girl appeared in my head. I had to rethink what I was doing. I was still

back home and that was it. I had to think about my choice again. I chose again—or let myself be chosen by—the religious path. It would be abnormal for this kind of thing not to happen."[17]

Notice that the future pope did not abandon the seminary, despite his strong feelings. But he did have to do some soul-searching. The prophet Jeremiah says, "There is nothing more tortuous than the human heart" (Jer 17:10).

Seminaries are careful to teach their men how to set appropriate boundaries with women, and how to guard their hearts and their vocations. If the seminarians follow the directives of their training, and if they are called to be priests, they will usually persevere. Seminarians are taught to be completely transparent with their spiritual director about every relationship and every area of their life. By keeping things "in the light," the seminarian will be able to correctly discern if falling in love with a particular woman is part of God's plan for him because he is called to marriage, or if he is still called to discern the priesthood.

Of course, a seminarian is free to leave the seminary at any time, for whatever reason. We ask seminarians to commit to one year at a time, but we cannot and would not try to stop them if they insist on leaving during the year.

Yes, the human heart can attach to another person, with or without permission!

"There are seven locks on the human heart, and the first always opens silently."

Ancient Proverb

What if a man falls in love after he is ordained? Will he be excommunicated if he decides to leave the priesthood and get married?

If a married man falls in love with his secretary at work, does that mean that he is not called to be married to his wife? No. In the same way, if a priest falls in love with a woman, it does not mean that he is not called to be a priest! However, when this happens—and we all know that it does happen from time to time—this priest will have a grave decision to make. There are no canonical consequences for a seminarian who leaves seminary to date and get married, as the seminarian has not made any permanent commitment to priesthood. However, once the man is ordained a deacon and makes his promise of celibacy, this all changes. A deacon or priest who leaves and gets married is in violation of his canonical promise. He is not able to receive Holy Communion and is in an irregular state, similar to a person who divorces and remarries outside of the Church. But he is not excommunicated! Excommunication is the most severe canonical penalty possible, and it is levied against people who, for example, intentionally desecrate the Eucharist, who try to kill the Pope, or commit other kinds of malicious, sacrilegious acts.

If a deacon or priest leaves active ministry for some reason, but does not get married, he is still in communion with the Church and can still practice his faith and receive Holy Communion. His promise of celibacy is still in effect, so he would not be able to date women. Analogously, he is still a married man, but living separately from his wife.

If a deacon or priest leaves active ministry to marry, he can petition Rome for a dispensation from his promise of celibacy. He can also apply for a *laicization*, the process of being returned to the lay state. Once a deacon or priest receives this laicization, and the dispensation from his promise of celibacy (which can only be granted by the Pope), he can marry in the Catholic Church and receive Holy Communion again. Laicization does not mean that this priest is no longer a priest. Once ordained, his soul is changed forever, marked with an indelible sign. He is still a priest and can even use his priestly powers in cases of emergency. For example, when a person is in danger of death, he can give the sacrament of anointing of the sick and absolution of their sins. However, he would no longer have the faculties from his bishop to function as a priest under ordinary circumstances.

If my son becomes a priest, what are the opportunities to climb the corporate ladder? How can he become a monsignor, a bishop, a cardinal, or even the pope?

Two of the apostles asked this same question:

"Then James and John, the sons of Zebedee, came to him and said to him, 'Teacher, we want you to do for us whatever we ask of you.' He replied, 'What do you wish your glory we may sit one at your right and the other at your left.' Jesus said to them, 'You do not know what you are asking. Can you drink the cup that I drink or be baptized with the baptism with which I am baptized?' They said to him, 'We can.' Jesus said to them, 'The cup that I drink, you will drink, and with the baptism with which I am baptized, you will be baptized; but to sit at my right or at my left is not mine to give but is for those for whom it has been prepared.' When the ten heard this, they became indignant at James and John. Jesus summoned them and said to them, 'You know that those who are recognized as rulers over the Gentiles lord it over them, and their great ones make their authority over them felt. But it shall not be so among you. Rather, whoever wishes to be great among you will be your servant; whoever wishes to be first among you will be the slave of all. For the Son of Man did not come to be served but to serve and to give his life as a ransom for many.'"

Mark 10:35-45

It is understandable why one would ask this question. Climbing the corporate ladder is a familiar and accepted objective in the business world, so if your son endeavors to be a priest, why not a bishop? But this concept does not and should not apply to priesthood. Priests are followers of Jesus Christ, who said, "whoever humbles himself will be exalted and whoever exalts himself will be humbled." Seminarians are taught to desire holiness. Ambition is discouraged as it is antithetical to the mission of the priest. Seeking power in the Church is an indication that a man desires priesthood for the wrong reasons.

"Some Christians — sometimes unconsciously — are after power. There are climbers in the Church! There are many who knock on the door of the Church, looking for some kind of advantage. But if you don't mind, head north and do some alpine climbing. It's healthier! Don't come to the Church to do your climbing!" [18]

Pope Francis

We stated earlier that there are only three levels in the sacrament of Holy Orders: deacon, priest, and bishop. These orders must be received in ascending order. If your son is studying to become a priest, then this is his goal and at his priestly ordination, he has reached that goal. Now his work is to serve the people of God as a priest.

A small percentage of priests are called by God through the Holy Father to serve as bishops. Yes, bishops possess much authority in the Church, and with that comes a certain amount of honor. But the office of bishop also comes with tremendous headaches and heartaches. Having the chief care of souls of every person in the diocese is a great weight and responsibility. Being a bishop today, especially in the U.S., is sometimes more like being the CEO of a large corporation. It is not an easy job, nor a desirable one, and seminarians and priests should not aspire to "climb this ladder." Bishops have little time for the great pastoral work of a priest: celebrating Mass, hearing confessions, visiting the sick, teaching the children, or caring for the poor. The administration of a diocese is time-consuming and difficult. The bishop is asked to do these things, always remembering that his primary duty is still to be the Chief Shepherd of God's people in his diocese.

What are monsignors and cardinals?

These are both simply honorary titles and they have been passed down through the tradition of the Church. "Monsignor" is an honorary title given to a priest by the Pope, at his bishop's request. It signifies that the priest has served the Church in an exemplary manner for many years. Most dioceses have some priests who have been honored with this title. However, being named a monsignor does not give that priest any more sacramental power than he had before. The change is more in address and dress. He is now typically addressed as "Monsignor" instead of "Father," and he is given more stately garments to wear. But there are still only three levels of Holy Orders.

Very recently, Pope Francis changed the guidelines under which priests can receive this honorary title. To be named a Monsignor, a priest must be at least sixty-five years old and have been a faithful priest for many years.

A cardinal is likewise an honorary title, but a much higher honor, which is usually given to an exemplary bishop directly by bishop any more sacramental power than he had before. He already possessed the fullness of the power of the priesthood as a bishop. However, cardinals do have much more administrative influence in the universal Church. They are usually named to papal commissions and they must travel to Rome for meetings many times per year. There is the change of address and dress. A cardinal receives a new title and is ordinarily referred to as "Your Eminence." He wears a bright red cassock and zucchetto (the small skull cap worn by bishops). Once a bishop has been admitted to the College of Cardinals, he attends the conclave to elect a new Pope unless he has reached eighty years of age before the conclave begins.

Are priests ever reprimanded by their bishops?

The bishop must sometimes call in a priest because of some action or behavior unbefitting a priest of Jesus Christ. Seminaries work hard to train their men to be good priests and to be conscious that the world is watching them. Being a priest is like living in a fish bowl. People watch what he does, listen to what he says, and repeat these things to others. Being a "public person" can be a difficult aspect of formation for some seminarians. For example, if a priest is using curse words or crude language on a regular basis, if he is outwardly angry and screams at people, if he is clearly struggling with an addiction to alcohol or drugs, if he is acting like "a bull in a china shop" in the parish, then he will get a call from the bishop or his delegate. Bishops love their priests as fathers love their sons, but they also love the People of God and have to be sure that the priest is treating people well. The priest will be encouraged (or even required) to seek counseling or treatment for the presenting issue. If the priest refuses to do what the bishop asks, he could be suspended and thus no longer able to function as a priest until he complies.

What happens if a priest violates one of his ordination promises?

Please recall that diocesan priests make three promises at their ordination. They promise to remain celibate for the sake of the Kingdom of God. They promise to pray faithfully the Liturgy of the Hours (the breviary or Divine Office) for God's people. And they promise respect and obedience to their bishops.

Obviously if a priest is having a romantic relationship with a woman, this is a violation of his promise and, once discovered, the bishop will have to intervene. The priest will have to choose either to be faithful to his promise of celibacy or to leave the active ministry. He will also need to deal with this sin in confession, though no one can force him to go to confession. If the affair becomes known publicly, the priest is often removed from active ministry.

If a priest is not praying the Breviary on a daily basis, this is also a violation of his promise and a matter for the confessional, though most bishops allow their priests to deal with this in spiritual direction. Bishops are priests too, and they understand how difficult it can be to maintain a viable prayer life with the amount of work required by their position. Bishops also know that prayer is essential if the man is to remain a good priest.

Finally, the promise of respect and obedience made by a priest to his bishop is one that comes into play throughout his life, most notably when the bishop assigns him to a new parish or job. The priest is to respect that promise and go where the bishop needs him, whether or not that is his own preference. But that promise also means that a priest is to cooperate with and to support the bishop in his pastoral leadership of the diocese. When a priest obstinately refuses to obey his bishop in any of these ways, he is doing something very sinful and is opening himself up to suspension.

Priests get sick, just like lay people get sick. Some priests struggle with depression or bi-polar disorder. Priests struggle with their own personal "demons" and sometimes these demons get the better of the fight. A bishop will reach out to these priests and get them help, if the priests are willing to be helped. There are special hospitals and treatment programs around the U.S. which specialize in rehabilitating priests and religious so that they can return to active ministry caring for God's people.

What type of ongoing formation will my son get after he is ordained a priest?

Ordination is not emancipation from formation. The first few years of priesthood are times of great learning for the newly ordained priest. It is the difference between studying theology in a book and practicing priesthood in the lives of real people! This is true of most professions, and it is certainly true in priesthood.

The newly ordained priest should be sent to assist the best pastors available, who will guide and assist them in how to handle the multitude of pastoral dilemmas.

Just as doctors, lawyers and teachers are required to undergo periodic updates regarding their profession, so priests also must participate in an annual week of continuing education. Many dioceses have an office for the continuing education of priests and they sponsor mandatory events like the Clergy Conference or Clergy Enrichment Days. These seminars will treat different topics in the life of a priest, such as Scripture, marriage preparation, personal health, time management, parish administration, etc. These continuing education seminars are normally mandatory for all priests and they are paid for either by the diocese or by the parish.

Some dioceses have a full time Vicar for Priests. This is a priest who spends all of his time working with the priests of the diocese on their specific issues and growth areas. Every priest is also strongly encouraged to have a spiritual director. This was required in the seminary, and it is very important to continue as a priest.

Finally, every seven years or so (this varies from diocese to diocese), a priest may request a sabbatical from his bishop in order to go rest, study, and be refreshed. These sabbaticals typically last from three to six months, and they often include classes updating the priest on issues in the Church. The bishop is not always able to grant these sabbaticals when they are requested, but he does his best as he very much desires that his priests remain healthy, happy, and current.

Once my son is a priest, will he be sent to the other side of the world so that I rarely see him?

If your son is studying for your home diocese, I have good news. Since he will be a diocesan priest, he almost always will be assigned within the geographical boundaries of your diocese. He is not likely to be sent to another state or another part of the world. His diocese, through the bishop, funded his education and priestly formation. He is "incardinated" in this diocese. He "belongs" to this diocese. He may be transferred from one parish to another within the diocese, but he will never be very far away, unless he is given a "specialized assignment."

What is a "specialized assignment?"

A small number of diocesan priests are given assignments outside a parish setting. These include special jobs within the diocese such as becoming the vocation director, vicar general, or chancellor, as well as assignments that require work outside the diocese. I myself received an assignment like this, when I was sent to work as the vice rector of a seminary located five hundred miles from my home.

A diocesan priest promises obedience to his bishop, and even though he always assumes that parish ministry will be his call, the Holy Spirit sometimes has other plans. I remember a conversation in which the mother of a newly assigned priest was asked: "So what do you think about your son, Fr. Smith, being given a special assignment in Rome, across the Atlantic Ocean?" The mother replied, "Well, I hate to see him go so far away, but he doesn't belong to me anymore. He belongs to Jesus and his Church."

As a priest, will my son be free to come help us, his parents, if we were to get sick or in case of a family emergency?

The answer is almost always yes. If you were to get sick, your son will certainly come to be with you and to do all that he can. Of course, he will still have parish responsibilities but other priests will cover his Masses for him during an emergency. This does not mean that a priest can just quit and go care for his sick parents for five years, but a priest does have great liberty in this regard. The bishop will usually do his best to reassign a priest closer to his ailing parents so that he can be more present.

How are priest assignments made? Will my son have any say in where he is sent to serve?

Every bishop has his own manner of making priest assignments, but most will at least discuss a potential assignment with the priest before making it final. There was a time in the Church when the priest simply received a letter, telling him where and when to go to his new assignment. Today, at least in the U.S., bishops usually discuss priest transfers with their Personnel Committee, trying very hard to match up the priest and the assignment well. Bishops, or their delegates, will then call the priest to discuss it, in case there are some unknown circumstances. Perhaps the priest has a specific medical condition and the doctor he needs is located in a particular city. All of these things will be duly considered, but sometimes the bishop still has to transfer the priest. This is where the promise of obedience is tested.

What if our son is going through a crisis of faith or doubting his vocation as a priest? What if he later regrets being a priest and giving up a wife and children? What role can we play that will help him?

Some priests do go through a vocation crisis after ordination, and it is important that they seek help. On becoming aware of this, parents can ask gently if he is discussing these things with his spiritual director, a brother priest, or the bishop. The answer to these questions often will be no. When a priest is in danger of losing his vocation and leaving the priesthood, it is very important that the bishop be made aware of this as soon as possible. The bishop will do all in his power to help this priest. He has many resources at his disposal. If you, as his parents, can act to get your son the help he needs and he is able to return to active ministry as a healthy, happy priest, many souls will potentially be affected. This is where we get the famous expression, "He who saves a priest saves a thousand souls!"

The Mother of Pope Saint Pius X

Pope Pius X was a very humble man and he had a saintly mother. Because they were so poor, she worked as a washer woman and a school janitor to earn enough money so that he could go to the seminary. In those days, the family had to pay for the seminarian's education. When elected pope, he was embarrassed and uncomfortable with the pomp and circumstance of the office. "Look how they have dressed me up," he lamented to a friend.

It is said that after his installation as pope, his mother kissed his large papal ring, as is the custom. She then presented her tiny hand with her wedding ring and said, "Now you kiss my ring — for without it, you never would have received yours!"

Chapter 11

HOW TO SUPPORT YOUR SEMINARIAN SON

Whether or not you are totally comfortable with your son's decision to go to seminary, I hope you can see by now that he really needs your support. We have spent a great deal of time describing the discernment process and seminary formation, both of which are very demanding. Parents have asked me through the years, "Okay, so my son is going to give seminary a try. What is my role now? How can I best support him?" Some of the following suggestions have already been mentioned, but they are included here again for emphasis.

Show Balanced Support

Do not put undue pressure on your son either to be a priest or not to be a priest. Some parents become very excited when they hear that their son is going to seminary. Here are the mistakes that some parents make. They call all their relatives and friends immediately and tell everyone that their son is going to become a priest. They start buying chalices and vestments when their son begins pre-theology — still six or eight years away from priesthood ordination. They constantly say things like, "When you are ordained a priest, you will…" This is often perceived as undue pressure. From reading this book, you already know that going to the seminary is not a final decision to become a priest. Much can happen. It might not work out. Parents should be supportive, but not overly exuberant. Reassure your son again and again that you love him and that you are proud of him for answering this call (as it is perceived presently). But tell him that you will be equally proud of him if God calls him to leave priestly formation and come home.

Learn about the discernment process

There are a number of resources available which young men use to discern priesthood. I recommend that parents — perhaps in a parent study group, or with immediate family members — read and discuss these resources. Some suggested resources can be found in the Recommended Reading appendix. You may also wish to read my previous book for young men: *To Save a Thousand Souls: A Guide for Discerning a Vocation to Diocesan Priesthood.*

Become knowledgeable about priestly formation and the life of a priest.

Seek good information to your questions, like you are doing now by reading this book, so that you can intelligently discuss with your son the process of priestly formation. I recently heard of a married couple who invited their son's vocation director to their home for dinner, specifically at a time when they knew their son would not be in town. They drilled this priest with questions for two hours! This is what I mean by proactively seeking good information.

Tell your son that you are proud of him and show awareness of the difficulty of discerning priesthood

Affirmation is an important parental virtue and it has very positive effects on children at all ages. Tell your son that you are proud of his goodness and generosity, whether or not he ends up becoming a priest. Most men have a tremendous struggle in discerning diocesan priesthood — whether or not to go to seminary, and when. It is very encouraging when parents understand that this process is so arduous!

Go visit the seminary

For many reasons already covered in this book, parents should visit their son's seminary, once per year if possible. Go to the "family weekend" offered by the seminary or by the diocese. Meet your son's professors, the rector, his spiritual director and his brother seminarians. Visit his room and show your sincere interest in the formation program. Your interest gives him great support!

Send care packages from home

Seminarians love to receive letters and "care packages" from their families and friends. I remember a seminary classmate of

Italian heritage who received the most wonderful care packages twice a month from his mother. I always helped him carry this package up to his room, as she made the best Italian cookies ever! I can also remember, as a seminary faculty member, watching seminarians go to the mail room, open their mailboxes and then slam them closed quickly with disappointed looks on their faces. I heard several remark through the years: "I have been here for three years and I have never received an encouraging letter or care package from anyone! I wonder if they even remember that I am here?"

Seminarians also love to receive letters and pictures from the students in Catholic schools or the Religious Education program, promising their prayers. When they come home, they can go and visit these classes to personally thank the children and to encourage them to consider priesthood. As a parent, you can facilitate this.

Maintain contact with the parents of other seminarians

With the social media network today, it is easy to maintain good relationships with the families of other seminarians from your diocese. Some dioceses have an email distribution list or a social media account where photos, updates, and information can be shared. Your knowledge of what is going on with the other seminarians in the diocese shows your support for your son and for the diocesan vocation program. Knowing who has left the program, how many new seminarians are coming in, who is being ordained this year, the initiatives of the vocation office, etc., keeps you as a parent aware of what is going on in your son's world.

In my diocese, the mothers of seminarians and priests meet together monthly, either physically or via the Internet, to pray for their sons. They send an email to all priests and seminarians before the meeting, to ask for their specific prayer intentions!

Join the Serra Club or another vocation promotion club

Many dioceses have a Serra Club or another club for the promotion of priestly and religious vocations. Serra Clubs exist solely to support vocations to the priesthood and religious life, and they do excellent work. The Knights of Columbus (though only for Catholic men) place a strong emphasis on vocations also.

Participating in these apostolates keeps parents very aware of the diocesan, national, and international vocation situation.

Welcome your son (and his friends) home for the holidays

Invite your son to come home at Thanksgiving, Christmas, and on other holidays. Make sure he feels welcome and still very much a part of the family. When he is home, ask him a lot of questions about his seminary formation, and his general well-being. This shows your interest and support. Because some seminarians live very far from the seminary, they are unable to go home for the shorter breaks. In a spirit of fraternal charity, seminarians will often invite these other seminarians to come home with them for the holidays. Get to know his friends from the seminary. Welcome them to your home!

Save the dates early!

Make sure you attend all of the Masses during which your son will receive the ministries of Lector, Acolyte, and Candidacy. By all means, be present and celebrate with him when he is ordained a deacon and then a priest! Put these dates on your calendar when you receive them and invite your relatives and friends early.

Keep in mind the analogy we have been using with courtship and marriage. Going to the seminary is like starting to date a girl exclusively. Finishing second theology, in some ways, is like becoming engaged. He is no longer discerning but preparing for the wedding — his ordination to the diaconate. Yet nothing permanent has happened yet. The diaconate ordination is a big deal during which your son's permanent commitments are first made. Once he is ordained a deacon, he has one more year before "he takes up residence with his bride." The ordination to priesthood is like the wedding feast! This is the greatest celebration of this entire process. An ordination reception is usually much more simple than a wedding reception, but the ordination and celebration are very important events. By keeping this analogy in mind, you will understand how to celebrate each of these smaller steps leading to the large steps of diaconate and priesthood.

"The pious soul prays not to inform God but to be conformed to His will."

St. Augustine

Pray for your son every day, and tell him that you are praying for him. While he is in the seminary, pray for his accurate discernment and perseverance. After he is ordained a priest, pray that he will be a holy priest. Pray that he will grow in faith, hope and love, so that he can be a powerful witness to others.

Finally, pray for his protection from evil in all its forms. A retreat master I once heard commented:

> "Satan paints a big target on the back of every priest on the day of his ordination. He knows that when a priest falls, he can take many people down with him. Satan can read Scripture: 'Strike the shepherd and the sheep will be scattered.' This is why it is so important for the People of God to pray for their priests!"

As I wrote in *To Save a Thousand Souls*, the ideal parents of a seminarian would communicate this attitude to their son:

> "I love you very much and I am proud of you for even considering priesthood. I will pray for you and support you as you go to the seminary. I will be very proud of you if you become a priest. But I will be equally proud of you if you discern that you must leave the seminary. I will welcome you home and help you in any way I can to find your true vocation. I am just proud that you love Jesus this much and that your faith is this strong."

Yes, be proud of your seminarian and priest-son but also make it clear that you are proud of all your children who are striving to live out their respective vocations.

Not every man is called to be a priest and receiving this call does not make one child better or more important than another. I remember this point very distinctly because of a conversation at a reception after a priestly ordination I attended. This priest was the only one ordained that year for that diocese, so he was receiving a lot of attention. There were hundreds of people there kindly expressing their congratulations to him and to his family. Towards the end of the night, we were all standing around with this newly ordained priest and his extended family. One of his pious aunts said to his mother, a comment she had doubtlessly heard a hundred times that day: "You must be so proud of your son, who is now a priest of Jesus Christ." His mother responded, glancing at all of his brothers and sisters standing around her:

> "Yes, I am proud of my priest-son, but I am equally proud of all of my children. They have all sought to do the will of God. I am proud of my married children as they are trying to live as God has called them and of my single children who are still seeking God's plan."

I was very proud of that mother. I thought to myself, "What a perfect response!" And I think her example is a good one for all parents of seminarians and priests.

"Jesus went around to all the towns and villages, teaching in their synagogues, proclaiming the gospel of the kingdom, and curing every disease and illness. At the sight of the crowds, his heart was moved with pity for them because they were troubled and abandoned, like sheep without a shepherd. Then he said to his disciples, 'The harvest is abundant but the laborers are few; so ask the master of the harvest to send out laborers for his harvest.'"

Matthew 9:35-37

Father's Dying Wish Was to See Son Ordained

Six months before his scheduled ordination to the priesthood, Deacon Richard Dyer of Arlington, Virginia, wrote an urgent letter to his bishop. In it, Richard described how his father was dying of kidney cancer, and probably would not live to see his son ordained a priest.

In a highly unusual accommodation, Bishop Paul Loverde ordained Richard to the priesthood six months early, on December 27, 2012. During the ordination Mass, Richard sat next to his father's wheelchair. "I just reached out and held my dad's hand," he said. "He was very sick, but aware of what was going on."

Immediately after he was ordained, Fr. Dyer gave his father his first blessing as a priest. "Something told me to do it then and not to wait until later," he said.

The ailing father was unable to attend Fr. Dyer's Mass of thanksgiving the next day. But just before he died, those caring for him said he seemed like he was trying to listen. "They said that he was really concentrating," Fr. Dyer said. "He was trying to be present at the Mass. He was perhaps receiving some grace to be there in a mysterious way."

Richard Dyer, Sr. passed away at almost the same time his son finished celebrating his first Mass.

"Even amongst the sadness, there's so much grace being poured out on me, my dad, and my family," Father Dyer said. "We do have our moments of sadness and deep sadness, of course, on the natural level, but because of our faith, we turn to Christ in hope of the Resurrection."

Fr. Dyer's first funeral Mass was for his father, Richard Dyer, Sr., who was laid to rest in Arlington National Cemetery.

Chapter 12

MY PRIEST SON, GOD'S WILL BE DONE

In Catholic tradition, there is an apocryphal story — not from inspired Gospel, but nonetheless enlightening — about when Jesus was a small boy living in Egypt. One day, his mother Mary was sitting at her weaving and the five-year-old Jesus was playing in the house. It was close to evening. As the sun was going down, its bright light shone through the open doorway. The little boy stood up and held his arms straight out on either side of him, fascinated by the shadow he was making on the wall. He said, "Look, Mamma! Look what I am doing!" Mary looked up and saw the shadow of a cross. She gasped, and then she began to cry. Jesus went to her and said, "Mamma, why are you crying? Why are you sad?" Mary hugged her son to her breast and she sobbed. Because in her heart, she knew.

It had all been prophesied five years before, when Jesus was only eight days old. Mary and Joseph had taken their newborn son to the Temple, to be presented and consecrated, ransomed for a pair of turtle doves. Simeon blessed the young parents and then, taking the child in his arms, he said to Mary, "Behold, this child is destined for the fall and rise of many in Israel, and to be a sign that will be contradicted. And you yourself a sword will pierce so that the thoughts of many hearts may be revealed" (Luke 3:33-35). Mary knew that she would have to suffer.

She knew the messianic prophecies. Every devout Jew studied these Scriptures. The prophets foretold that the Messiah was to be tortured, crucified, and put to death. But did she know that Jesus was the Messiah? Look at how her life had unfolded. Mary remembered the visit of the Angel Gabriel when she became pregnant by the Holy Spirit. How could she ever forget such a meeting? He said, "Do not be afraid Mary, for you have found favor with God. Behold, you will conceive in your womb and bear a son, and you shall name him Jesus. He will be great and will be called Son of the Most High." She replied in obedience and faith, "May it be done to me according to your word."

Mary had all of these memories in her heart. There may have been many times in her young boy's life when she hugged him tightly and cried. She would have prayed for grace and strength to be there for him always.

And she was there for him, as the Gospel of John tells us: "Standing by the cross of Jesus were his mother and his mother's sister" (John 19:25). The more accurate translation is: "She *kept on standing* beneath the cross."

Jesus is *the* High Priest, the Son of God and Savior of the world. He is the only true priest. He offered himself on the altar of the cross once and for all two thousand years ago and he offers himself again every time the Holy Mass is celebrated. Every priest today stands in the place of Christ, and offers this same sacrifice. And yes, priests are asked to make sacrifices for the salvation of God's people, just like the Master.

And the parents of priests are asked to make sacrifices with him, just like Mary and Joseph. If your son becomes a priest, hundreds of thousands of people will be fed with the Body and Blood of Jesus Christ through his hands!

Mary had no grandchildren. Did this ever occur to you? I am sure that, like every other mother, she would have loved to have held her son's children. But it was not the plan of God for her, just as marriage was not the plan of God for her son. Yet Mary is called "Mother" by billions. She is called Mother of God, most blessed among all women.

What about St. Joseph? He certainly deserves credit also. Though not the biological father of Jesus, he was still his father. Joseph taught the "God-Child" how to pray and to be a child of God; and he taught the "God-Man" how to be a man! He taught Jesus how to work hard and to persevere in trials.

The Blessed Mother and St. Joseph are the perfect patron saints for the parents of priests.

"Every vocation to the priesthood comes from the heart of God, but it passes through the heart of the mother."

Pope St. Pius X

Based on my experience, many parents of aspiring priests may feel uneasy, but the parents of long-ordained priests experience much joy. What is so great about having a priest in the family?

It is the will of God

If being a priest of Jesus Christ is God's plan for the life of your son, then this is what a parent should want also. It is the best plan for his happiness and salvation. The prayer I recommend is: *"God, I want to want what you want. Even if I don't want it, I want to want it."*

Whether or not it makes you uncomfortable to consider it, having a "priest-son" usually indicates that you did a lot of things right in raising him. In humility, you can acknowledge the truth that God did most of the work in calling your son to be a priest—but you did your part also. It is perfectly acceptable to feel good about having parented your son well. You can rightfully feel a measure of pride when realizing that your son is being used by God to do so much good for others. Like the Blessed Mother, a priest's parent can say, "Thy will be done."

Priests are respected and loved

While priesthood may not be highly regarded by society at large, priests are respected and loved by the people in their parishes. Even non-believers sometimes have a begrudging admiration of a priest's obvious dedication to what he believes in. Even with the terrible press about some priests, the people of God know that their priest stands in the place of Jesus. He is a very important person, a true father, to many people. To see their son so well-regarded by so many people is a great joy to parents.

The family priest

It is great to have a priest in the family when it is time for family baptisms, First Confessions, First Holy Communions, Confirmations, weddings, and funerals. It is true that a priest is a part of every family, precisely because he is with every family during these important moments. Even still, it is extra special to have your "own" priest when it is time for these family occasions.

A priest *is* a part of every family. I often marvel that on any given day, I could get into my car and drive to any one of a thousand homes and ring the doorbell unexpected; and I would be welcomed by that family and usually invited to dinner! Why would I be so welcome? Because as a priest, I stand in the place of Jesus. Catholics love Jesus, therefore they love their priests!

"To live in the midst of the world with no desire for its pleasures; to be a member of every family, yet belonging to none; to share all sufferings; to penetrate all secrets, to heal all wounds; to daily go from men to God to offer Him their homage and petitions; to return from God to men to bring them His pardon and hope; to have a heart of fire for charity and a heart of bronze for chastity; to bless and to be blest forever. O God, what a life, and it is yours, O Priest of Jesus Christ!"

Jean-Baptiste Henri Lacordaire, O.P. (1802-1861)

Expert Catholic answers

Every Catholic family will sometimes have questions and concerns about some teaching of the Church, the latest news from the Holy Father in Rome, or things that are happening at the diocesan level with the local bishop. Having a priest-son always gives you a confidential and safe place to go for expert answers to spiritual and ecclesial questions.

Home Masses

On his day off, while on vacation, or when home for the holidays, your priest-son can celebrate Masses in your home for your intentions, for example, or for deceased friends and family members. Your priest-son will be present with you at nearly every holiday celebration, since he does not have to alternate with the in-laws. I remember with joy the many family Masses at the dining room table with my parents, siblings, and all of my little nieces and nephews! I can still see them all kneeling around the table during the Eucharistic Prayer and I prayed in my heart, "Jesus, please bring us all to Heaven where we will share together the Heavenly Banquet."

Comfort at the end of life

Generally speaking, I have found that as parents get older and closer to their own deaths and judgments, they become more peaceful and happy that their son is a priest, however they may have felt at the beginning. When parents get old and sick, it is a great comfort to have a priest-son, an "expert in the spiritual life," sitting by your bed. It is a consolation to receive the powerful sacraments of the dying—the Last Rites of Confession, Holy Communion and Anointing of the Sick—directly from the hands of your son. It is a wonderful grace to receive the Apostolic Pardon at the moment of death from the lips of your own flesh and blood, as he raises his hand in blessing and says: *"Through the holy mysteries of our redemption, may almighty God release you from all punishments in this life and in the life to come. May he open to you the gates of paradise and welcome you to everlasting joy. Amen."*

God's call to parents through his call to their sons

You may have heard the aphorism that faith is caught, not taught. God designed marriage and family so that the gift of faith would be passed down from one generation to the next. Though faith is always a gift from God, small children receive it almost always through their mothers and fathers.

I have noticed that it also works the other way around. The father of a priest in Virginia said it well: "The Sacrament of Holy Orders has had a 'halo effect' on me, my wife, and my other children and grandchildren. We cannot help but feel closer to Jesus because of our son's vocation as a priest."

Parents, did it ever occur to you that one of the reasons God has called your son to be a priest is so that your own faith will be strengthened? All of our vocations are interconnected. It was your commitment to the vocation of marriage that brought your son into this world; it very well may be that his commitment to the vocation of priesthood may help bring you into the next world.

As this book comes to an end, I want to propose a very important question: What is God calling *you* to do, through his call to your son to be a priest?

Is God calling you to improve your faith life by attending daily Mass, by praying a daily rosary, or by going to a Holy Hour (a one-hour time of adoration of Jesus in the Blessed Sacrament)?

If you are Catholic but away from the Church, would you consider returning? Is God calling you to return to Confession and Holy Communion? Is God calling you to get your faith life in order so that you can support your son?

If you are not Catholic, would you be willing to enroll in RCIA and at least learn about the Church's teachings from the source? Perhaps through God's call to your son, he is calling you to study the Catholic faith in its entirety.

What is God calling *you* to do, through his call to your son to go to seminary? Will you answer this call, just as your son is answering his?

A Happy Ending

"After the sabbath, as the first day of the week was dawning, Mary Magdalene and the other Mary came to see the tomb. And behold, there was a great earthquake; for an angel of the Lord descended from heaven, approached, rolled back the stone, and sat upon it. His appearance was like lightning and his clothing was white as snow. The guards were shaken with fear of him and became like dead men. Then the angel said to the women in reply, 'Do not be afraid! I know that you are seeking Jesus the crucified. He is not here, for he has been raised just as he said. Come and see the place where he lay. Then go quickly and tell his disciples, "He has been raised from the dead, and he is going before you to Galilee; there you will see him." Behold, I have told you.' Then they went away quickly from the tomb, fearful yet overjoyed, and ran to announce this to his disciples."

Matthew 28:1-8

I would like to end this chapter as I began it, by recounting an apocryphal story about the life of Jesus, that while not Gospel truth, is highly plausible. Pope St. John Paul II mentioned this traditional story on several occasions during Easter Masses. He speculated that after Jesus rose from the dead early on Sunday morning, before he appeared to anyone else, he first appeared to his mother Mary. In all of the Scriptural Resurrection narratives, the faithful Mother of Jesus is never mentioned as being present. Many of the saints believe this would have been impossible given her great love and devotion to Jesus. She most certainly would have accompanied the other holy women who went to the tomb with perfume to anoint the body of the Lord... Unless Jesus had already first appeared to her privately!

Can you imagine the joy that the Blessed Mother would have experienced when she saw the risen Jesus clothed in glory? After all the pain and suffering she endured in supporting the vocation of her son, she saw that the prophecies had come true. Christ had risen! Mary would have hugged her son and sobbed, much as she may have done when he was a small boy.

God loves all of his children so much that he sent his son to suffer, to die, and to rise, so that the Gates of Heaven would be opened to all. Now he sends out workers to bring in the harvest. If your son is called to be a priest, he will bring Jesus to the world in a powerful way. Like the Blessed Mother Mary and St. Joseph, you, parents, have done your part in bringing Jesus to the world. *And you still have an important part to play.* I hope you can thank God that he may be calling your son to be a priest.

Christianity always has a happy ending!

"Behold, I make all things new."
Revelation 21:5

*If this book has been helpful for you,
please consider making a donation to
The Foundation for Priestly Vocations,
which helps young men and their parents
remain open to the priesthood:*

www.VocationFoundation.org

A Prayer for My Seminarian Son

Father in Heaven, I thank you for my seminarian son.

Thank you for honoring him by calling him to be a priest.

Please grant him the gift of discernment, so that he will hear your voice clearly and do whatever You tell him.

Protect my son from all evil and danger, as he pursues this great good.

Lord Jesus, our High Priest, please help him to persevere in his vocation and to grow into your Divine Image.

And give me the grace to do my part as his parent: to walk with him, to support him, and to love him.

Lord God, I thank you for this great gift, to have a priest in the family.

Amen

INDEX OF QUESTIONS

Chapter 1: "Mom and Dad, I Have Great News

Chapter 2: Why Would Anyone Want to Be a Priest?

Chapter 3: What Exactly Does a Priest Do?

Chapter 4: Left Mending the Nets

Chapter 7: Applying to Seminary

Chapter 8: What Is Seminary Like?

37. What do seminarians do during the summers? Page 82

38. What are the three primary ministries which a man must receive as he proceeds towards priestly ordination? Page 82

39. At what point does a man make the three life-long promises to live celibacy for the sake of the Kingdom of God, to pray the Liturgy of the Hours faithfully, and to show respect and obedience to his bishop? Page 82-83

40. At what point during this lengthy period of study and formation is a man ordained a deacon and then a priest? Page 83

Chapter 9: Who Is Paying for All of This?

41. If my son leaves the seminary, will he have to pay back the money the diocese spent on his education? Page 87

42. Does the diocese support the seminarians monetarily while they are in seminary, or do the families have to support them? Page 88

43. What does a man do if he has student loans to repay? Page 89

44. If he needs money, can a seminarian hold a job while in the seminary? Page 89

45. Will he be permitted to get a summer job to make some extra money? Page 90

46. Do seminarians get a vacation? Once ordained, do priests get a vacation and time off on a regular basis? Who pays for this vacation? Page 90

47. How do diocesan priests get paid? Will he need financial support from his family? Page 91

48.

49. Do seminarians and priests have good health insurance, and who pays for it? Page 92

50. How and when can a priest retire? Where do they go? Pages 92-93

62. If my son becomes a priest, what are the opportunities to climb the corporate ladder? How can he become a monsignor, a bishop, a cardinal or even the pope? Pages 105-107

63. What are monsignors and cardinals? Page 107

64. Are priests ever reprimanded by their bishops? Can a priest be fired? Page 108

65. What happens if a priest violates one of his ordination promises? Page 108

66. What type of ongoing formation will my son get after he is ordained a priest? Pages 109-110

67. Once my son is a priest, will he be sent to the other side of the world so that I rarely see him? Page 110

68. What is a "specialized assignment" for a diocesan priest? Page 110-111

69. As a priest, will my son be free to come help us, his parents, if we were to get sick or in case of a family emergency? Page 111

70. How are priest assignments made? Will my son have any say in where he is sent to serve? Page 111

71. What if our son is going through a crisis of faith or doubting his vocation as a priest? What if he later regrets being a priest and giving up a wife and children? What role can we play that will help him? Page 112

Chapter 11: How to Support Your Seminarian Son

72. How can I best support my seminarian son? Page 115-ff

73. Are parents and family members permitted to go and visit their son while he is in the seminary? Page 116

74. What would be the attitude of the ideal parent of a seminarian? Page 119

Chapter 12: My Priest Son, God's Will Be Done

RECOMMENDED READING

Vocation Discernment

Personal Vocation: God Calls Everyone By Name
Dr. Germain Grisez and Russell Shaw

What Does God Want
Fr. Michael Scanlon

Discovering Your Personal Vocation
Herbert Alphonso, S.J.

Is Jesus Calling You To Be A Catholic Priest? A Helpful Guide
Msgr. Thomas Richter, published by the NCDVD

Radical Surrender; Letters to Seminarians
Fr. Michael Najim

Paths of Love: The Discernment of Vocation According to the Teaching of Aquinas, Ignatius, and Pope John Paul II
Joseph Bolin

Could You Ever Become a Catholic Priest?
Christopher J. Duquin & Lorene Hanley Duquin

Called by Name: The Inspiring Stories of 12 Men Who Became Catholic Priests
Christine Mugridge

Priesthood

Priests for the Third Millennium
Archbishop Timothy Dolan

The Priest is Not His Own
Archbishop Fulton J. Sheen, 2004

Those Mysterious Priests
Archbishop Fulton J. Sheen, 2005

The Joy of Priesthood
Msgr. Stephen Rossetti

Reclaiming our Priestly Character
Fr. David Toups

Maurice and Therese: The Story of a Love
Saint Therese of Lisieux

Short Catechism on the Priesthood
St. John Vianney

The Grace of Ars
Fr. Frederick Miller

Together on the Road: A Vision of Lived Communion for the Church and the Priesthood
Massimo Camisasca

Dear Father: A Message of Love to Priests
Catherine De Hueck Doherty

Be Holy! God's First Call to Priests Today
Thomas Forrest, C.Ss.R.

A Celebration of Priestly Ministry: Challenge, Renewal, and Joy in the Catholic Priesthood
Cardinal Walter Kasper

Celibacy

The Courage to be Chaste
Fr. Benedict Groeschel

When God Asks for an Undivided Heart
Fr. Andrew Apostoli

Sacerdotalis Caelibatus (Priestly Celibacy)
Pope Paul VI, 1967

Virginity
Fr. Raniero Cantalamessa

"*...And You are Christ's*" *The Charism of Virginity and the Celibate Life*
Thomas Dubay, S.M.

Biographies or Autobiographies of Priests

Parish Priest: Father Michael McGivney and American Catholicism
Douglas Brinkley and Julie M. Fenster

The Cure D'Ars: St. Jean-Marie-Baptiste Vianney
F. Trochu

A Priest Forever
Fr. Benedict Groeschel

He Leadeth Me
Fr. Walter J. Ciszek, S.J.

Edmund Campion
Evelyn Waugh

From Slave to Priest: A Biography of the Reverend Augustine Tolton (1854 - 1897): First Black American Priest of the United States
Caroline Hemesath

Treasure in Clay
Archbishop Fulton Sheen

The Grunt Padre
Fr. Daniel Mode

A Shepherd in Combat Boots: Chaplain Emil Kapaun of the 1st Cavalry Division
William L. Maher

Holy Man: Father Damien of Molokai
Gavan Daws

The Shadow of His Wings: The True Story of Fr. Gereon Goldmann, OFM
Gereon Karl Goldmann

NOTES

[1] http://www.lanacion.com.ar/1564076-el-extasis-familiar-por-el-loco-de-la-

[2] Stephen J. Rossetti, *Ten Steps to Priestly Holiness: Our Journey into Joy* (Notre Dame: Ave Maria Press), 26

[3] http://www.usccb.org/beliefs-and-teachings/vocations/ordination-class/upload/Ordination-Class-of-2013-report-FINAL.pdf

[4] Lawrence G. Lovasik, S.V.D., Treasury of Catechism Stories (Pittsburg, PA: Marian Action Publictaions, 1966)

[5] http://www.zenit.org/en/articles/study-most-priests-are-happy-appreciate-celibacy

[6] http://www.catholic.com/tracts/celibacy-and-the-priesthood

[7] Friedrich Nietzsche, *Die fröhliche Wissenschaft*, 5.358

[8] *Gaudium et Spes*, 22

[9] Fr. Andrew Carl Wisdom, O.P., *Why Should I Encourage My Son To Be A Priest?* (Liguori, MO: Liguori)

[10] C.S. Lewis, *Mere Christianity* (New York: Touchstone), pp 170-171.

[11] Sam Alzheimer, *Vocation Mythbusters for Parents* (Valdosta, GA: Vianney Vocations)

[12] St. Thérèse of Lisieux, *The Story of a Soul: the Autobiography of St. Therese of Lisieux*, ed. Rev. T.N. Taylor (London: Burns, Oates & Washbourne, 1912; 8th ed., 1922)

[13] Jeanne Kun, *My Heart Speaks; Wisdom from Pope John XXIII* (Ijamsville, MD: The Word Among Us Press)

[14] Pope Benedict XVI, *Jesus of Nazareth* (New York: Doubleday)

[15] Francis Xavier Nguyen Van Thuan, *Testimony of Hope: The Spiritual Exercises of Pope John Paul II* (Boston: Pauline Books and Media)

[16] Pope John Paul II, *Pastores Dabo Vobis*

[17] Abraham Skorka, *Sobre el Cielo y la Tierra* (Sudamericana)

[18] Pope Francis, from a homily on May 5, 2014